ECERS-E
The Four Curricular Subscales Extension to the
Early Childhood Environment Rating Scale (ECERS-R)

4th Edition with Planning Notes

KATHY SYLVA **IRAM SIRAJ-BLATCHFORD** **BRENDA TAGGART**

Foreword by Thelma Harms

Teachers College, Columbia University
New York and London

This publication was first developed as part of the Effective Provision of Pre-school Education (EPPE) project and longitudinal study funded by U.K. Government. The study followed the development of a large sample of children from 3 years to age 16 (see U.K.s Department for Education research website at http://www.dfe.gov.uk/research). For information on EPPE, EPPE 3-11, EPPSE 3-14 and EPPSE 16+ visit http://eppe.ioe.ac.uk

Published by Teachers College Press, 1234 Amsterdam Avenue, New York, NY 10027

ISBN 978-0-8077-5150-3

Printed on acid-free paper

Manufactured in the United States of America

18   17   16   15   14   13   12   11   8   7   6   5   4   3   2   1

Contents

Foreword

The authors of the *Early Childhood Environment Rating Scale* are pleased to welcome the *Curricular Extension* to the ECERS-R, commonly referred to as the ECERS-E, to our family of Environment Rating Scales. Having a published version of the ECERS-E in the United States will facilitate access to this valuable extension to our ECERS-R for use both in our country and abroad.

A brief explanation of why and how the ECERS-E was developed will help to explain its relationship to the ECERS-R. The ECERS-E was developed, not as a replacement for the ECERS-R, but as an *expansion* of several items contained in the ECERS-R. The research team in England responsible for developing the ECERS-E was using the ECERS-R in a project called the Effective Provision of Pre-School Education (EPPE) Project. The purpose of the EPPE project was to identify preschool/kindergarten approaches that prepared children for success in primary school. The English research team was aware that, with the increased emphasis on school readiness, it had become extremely important to ensure that the teaching approaches used with young children to promote literacy, mathematics, and science resist the tendency to become rigid and academic. Recognizing that high-quality early childhood educational settings could provide preschool- and kindergarten-aged children with developmentally appropriate activities to introduce the basic skills that prepare them for later success in school, the authors of the ECERS-E expanded several items included in the ECERS-R, with the authors' approval, into complete subscales as an extension to be used with the ECERS-R, hence the title ECERS-E. The ECERS-R items that were expanded into these supplementary subscales include the four Language-Reasoning items, as well as the Math/Number, Nature/Science, and Promoting Acceptance of Diversity items.

The ECERS-E has been revised and improved as a result of its use in various research and program improvement projects. It was designed to be used along with the ECERS-R in the EPPE project in England in 1997–2003. It was published in England in 2003 as a research edition, and subsequently revised for publication in 2006. The current 2010 edition, published by Teachers College Press, renamed the *ECERS-E: The Four Curricular Subscales Extension to the Early Childhood Environment Rating Scale (ECERS)*, contains further revisions and expanded notes that will make it more user-friendly in the United States and in other countries.

The authors of the ECERS-E have continued to use this instrument along with the ECERS-R, which provides a more global, comprehensive assessment of program quality, as they continue their research and program improvement efforts in the United Kingdom. Professionals in the early childhood field in the United States and other countries are also finding the combination of the ECERS-R and the ECERS-E to be useful in assessing how well programs are meeting the three basic needs of children: protection of health and safety, support and guidance for social/emotional development, and appropriate activities to stimulate language and cognitive development. We are hopeful that the use of these two related instruments will continue to facilitate the provision of engaging and productive learning environments for young children worldwide.

Thelma Harms, PhD,
Lead author of *Early Childhood Environment Rating Scale-Revised*
University of North Carolina at Chapel Hill, 2010

Acknowledgments

Many people have contributed to the development and testing of this instrument and they have been acknowledged in earlier editions. For the development of this publication we are indebted to Sandra Mathers and Faye Linskey of A+ Education Ltd. (*see* www.aplus-education.co.uk). Through their training courses with advisory and practitioner groups, as well as work in assisting U.K. Local Authorities to use ECERS for measuring and improving quality, they have become experts on the scales. We have benefited from their expertise in expanding the notes for clarification. This was done by listening to the views of those who work every day with young children, collected from hundreds of field visits. Sandra and Faye have a unique and powerful blend of research experience coupled with practitioner knowledge. They will continue to be involved with the scales by developing the *All About the ECERS-E*. We are grateful to them both for their diligence, fine attention to detail, and, most importantly, their imaginative approach to assessment.

Kathy Sylva, Iram Siraj-Blatchford, and Brenda Taggart
August 2010

Principal Investigators of the EPPE Research Project

Professor Kathy Sylva
Department of Education, University of Oxford

Professor Edward Melhuish
Institute for the Study of Children, Families and Social Issues, Birkbeck, University of London

Professor Pam Sammons
Department of Education, University of Oxford

Professor Iram Siraj-Blatchford
Institute of Education, University of London

Brenda Taggart
Institute of Education, University of London

Introduction to the ECERS-E

The original Environment Rating Scales were developed in the United States by Thelma Harms, Dick Clifford, and Debby Cryer of the Frank Porter Graham Child Development Institute at the University of North Carolina, Chapel Hill. This curricular extension to the ECERS-R, or the ECERS-E as it has become known, belongs to a "family" of scales developed to assess provision for children aged 0 to 12 years. The "family" includes:

- *Infant/Toddler Environment Rating Scale–Revised* (ITERS-R), designed to assess group programs for children from birth to 2½ years of age (Harms, Clifford, & Cryer, 2005)
- *Early Childhood Environment Rating Scale–Revised* (ECERS-R), which assesses center-based provision for children from 2½ to 5 years of age (Harms, Clifford, & Cryer, 2005)
- *School-Age Care Environment Rating Scale* (SACERS), which assesses group-care for school-age children 5–12 years of age (Harms, Jacobs, & White, 1996)
- *Family Child Care Environment Rating Scale–Revised* (FCCERS-R), designed to assess family child-care programs conducted in a provider's home for children from infancy through school age (Harms, Cryer, & Clifford, 2007).

For more information on the ERS, visit: www.fpg.unc.edu/~ECERS/.

The American ECERS-R is a highly respected tool for research, self-evaluation, auditing, and inspection. It is used extensively in the United States both for state-wide audits to monitor program quality and for the training of early-years practitioners. Its international reputation is impressive, and it has been used in more than 20 countries, from Singapore to Chile. It has been translated and used extensively in Germany (Tietze et al., 1996) and in the United Kingdom (Sylva et al., 1999). In India (Ilsley, 2000) and China (Yan Yan & Yuejuan, 2008) researchers have used the ECERS-R as a conceptual template on which to build a very different assessment system designed to suit environments and practices which are far removed from the U.S. Early Childhood settings for which ECERS was first developed.

All those who have used the ECERS-R, and those new to the scales, will find the ECERS-E an essential addition to this suite of rating scales. This is especially true in the U.S. context, where there is an increasing emphasis on fostering sound emerging literacy and numeracy skills in young children. Using the ECERS-E alongside the ECERS-R gives U.S. users a more complete picture of what a high-quality Early Childhood Education (ECE) program can look like.

The U.S. emphasis on early literacy and math, along with the increasing concern for early science and environmental learning and the inclusion of all children in ECE programs, connects directly to the curricular assessments found in the ECERS-E. Current trends in U.S. ECE programs dovetail well with the material covered by this Fourth Edition of the ECERS-E. In addition, the section on planning will be of particular interest to U.S. colleagues. While most U.S. settings already post a daily/weekly schedule, mostly for parents' benefit, the ECERS-E provides an opportunity to consider a more in-depth approach to planning. This approach puts the individual child at the heart of the process, and will therefore be of considerable interest to U.S. early-years workers who wish to improve this aspect of their practice.

The ECERS-E has been used in many contexts outside the United Kingdom and has proved to be a popular and reliable tool. Members of the Frank Porter Graham Child Development Institute at the University of North Carolina, Chapel Hill, who have used the ECERS-E alongside of the ECERS-R in the United States have found the ECERS-E to be highly relevant to U.S. settings. It both complements and extends the ECERS-R.

ECERS-E: The Four Curricular Subscales Extension to the Early Childhood Environment Rating Scale (ECERS-R) was first developed for use in the United Kingdom through a prestigious research project: The Effective Provision of Pre-School Education (EPPE) study, which ran from 1997 to 2003. This longitudinal study, funded by the U.K. Government (*see* http://eppe.ioe.ac.uk), needed measures of preschool quality that were rigorous for research and also had credibility within the practitioner community. The adoption of the ECERS-R was uncontested, but the EPPE team needed to extend this into contexts more suited to England's developing frameworks for early-years education and care. The ECERS-R, developed in the 1980s, was based broadly on notions of Developmentally Appropriate Practice (DAP). It adopted a light touch in assessing the environment for developing children's emerging literacy, numeracy, and scientific thinking. Moreover, it is also light on assessing the environment aimed at understanding cultural and intellectual diversity. The ECERS-E seeks to supplement the ECERS-R in ways that reflected the *English Curriculum Guidance for the Foundation Stage* (Qualification and Curriculum Authority [QCA], 2000) as well as changing the notions of Developmentally Appropriate Practice, especially as these relate to emerging literacy, numeracy, scientific thinking, and diversity. Since the development of the ECERS-E, it has become an inseparable companion to the ECERS-R in the United Kingdom, the United States, and beyond. The two scales complement each other with only slight overlap.

The ECERS-E assesses the curriculum and environment for children 3 to 5 years old in the following areas:

- Literacy
- Mathematics
- Science/Environment
- Diversity (Race, Gender, and Individual Learning Needs)

The items in these subscales assess the quality of curricular provisions, including pedagogy, in those domains aimed at fostering children's academic development (Sammons et al., 2002).

The analyses of the EPPE data (which followed the progress and development of approximately 3,000 children from 3 to 11 years old; see Sylva et al., 2004, 2010) revealed the ECERS-E to be a better predictor of children's intellectual and language progress (3–5 years old) than assessments of the same settings using the ECERS-R. Scores on the total ECERS-R were not related to cognitive progress over the 2-year period, but the scores on its "Social Interaction" subscale were positively related to increases in children's **independence** and **cooperation**.

For academic development, however, the ECERS-E was significantly related to progress in children's **language, non-verbal reasoning, number skills,** and **pre-reading skills**. We suggest that quality is not a universal concept, but depends on national priorities to a large extent. If academic achievement is valued at the start of school, then the ECERS-E is a good predictor of readiness for school. But if social outcomes are valued, then the "Social Interaction" scale on the ECERS-R may be a better predictor of readiness. However, we strongly believe both are important and therefore recommend that the scales be used together. This is particularly important when using ECERS to monitor quality across a range of different curricular frameworks. We recommend using the ECERS-E alongside the ECERS-R for a more global assessment of quality. Centers in the United States that are familiar with the ECERS-R will find the ECERS-E a sympathetic and intuitive instrument. It will help to foster richer environments in which young children can flourish, especially in intellectual domains.

In England, all early childhood settings are inspected regularly by a regulatory body called The Office for Standards in Education (Ofsted). This is a national body that operates across the whole of England, with statutory powers to inspect and report on all types of settings that cater to the education of children (child care workers in centers and homes, early-years centers, schools, etc.). Ofsted is responsible for standards across a wide range of outcomes. It is responsible for monitoring health and safety standards, as well as ensuring the educational content of programs. There is no such national body equivalent in the United States, as inspection services are the responsibilities of individual states, but many of the individual state inspection programs contain areas of responsibility that are common across U.S. and U.K. inspection services (e.g., safety, access to learning activities, etc.).

In England, early childhood settings are inspected regularly, and prior to the inspection they are required to complete a document that is used during the inspection to determine the quality of the setting. When preparing for an Ofsted inspection, center managers and their staff have found both the ECERS-R and the ECERS-E useful in preparing a particular part of the document called the Self Assessment Form (SEF, see Office for Standards in Education [Ofsted], 2008). This requires centers to reflect on what they do to support children's learning. Although specific to the U.K. context, some sections of the SEF will resonate well in the U.S. and other settings. Any childhood setting, in any country, may wish to reflect on how well they support children under the following headings taken from the U.K.'s SEF. How well does your center accomplish the following?:

The learning and development of the children in the early years
- support learning in interactions with children
- plan the learning environment to help children progress towards early learning goals
- plan children's play with a balance of adult-led and child-led activities to help children to think critically and be active and creative learners
- plan for individual needs

The welfare of children in the early years
- help children to develop skills for the future
- how effective is the setting's self evaluation, including the steps taken to promote improvements?

The overall effectiveness of the early years
- how does the setting maintain continuous improvement?

Any center in any country that is using the ECERS-R and ECERS-E should be encouraged to reflect on this list—we believe the broad areas outlined above are relevant to all those involved in self-evaluation.

The ECERS-E and ECERS-R have been used extensively over the last 10 years as reliable and credible measures of quality in U.K. research. They have also been used in the United States by members of the Frank Porter Graham Child Development Institute at the University of North Carolina, Chapel Hill, and across a number of other countries (e.g., China, Australia, Greece, Portugal). They have been used in the United Kingdom on the following high profile studies (as well as a number of smaller research projects):

The Effective Pre-school Provision in Northern Ireland (EPPNI):
    www.deni.gov.uk/researchreport41-2.pdf
The Millennium Cohort Study (MCS):
    www.cls.ioe.ac.uk/studies.asp?section=000100020001
The National Evaluation of the Neighbourhood Nurseries Initiative:
    www.dfe.gov.uk/research/data/uploadfiles/SSU2007FR024.pdf
The National Evaluation of Sure Start:
    www.ness.bbk.ac.uk/
The Monitoring and Evaluation of the Effective Implementation of the Foundation Phase (MEEIFP) Project Across Wales:
    www.327matters.org/Docs/meeifp.pdf
Evaluation of the Early Education Pilot for Two-Year-Old Children (2006–2009): www.dfe.gov.uk/research/data/uploadfiles/DCSF-RR134.pdf
Evaluation of the Graduate Leader Fund (2007–2011):
    http://www.education.ox.ac.uk/research/resgroup/fell/cfellrp.php

Assessing Practice Related to a "Foundation" Curriculum for the Early Years

Many different curricula are appropriate for early childhood settings. All of them are based on models of child development and on ways that culture and society (through families, educational or childcare settings, and communities) shape the growing child. Some curricula make their theoretical basis very clear (e.g., High Scope, the Creative Curriculum, Tools of the Mind), while others rest on practice-based models of children's development and culture and ways to nurture it. The ECERS-E was not developed with any one curriculum in mind; the principles beneath the assessment of practice are drawn from child psychology and social, cultural, and educational practice. The ECERS-E authors come from a background of psychology, sociology, and early childhood education—and all three disciplines were drawn upon when devising the items and indicators. Hundreds of practitioners contributed to the development of the scales, along with social scientists, both in the United Kingdom and in the United States (making this extension particularly appropriate for U.S. settings).

We had much experience applying the ECERS-R (Harms et al., 2005) in England for research purposes and were convinced of its validity in providing a broad-brush assessment of practice (on a 7-point scale) in group education and care settings. However, the English government began developing a new curriculum in the mid-1990s for children 3–5+ years old, with specific domains related to "Communication, Language, and Literacy," "Mathematical Development," and "Knowledge and Understanding of the World." After consulting with an advisory group of English early childhood professionals, we decided that the ECERS-R might be supplemented by four curricular subscales (including "Diversity") to provide a robust measure of the kinds of educational practices in England that most experts believed were shaping cognitive development.

As researchers of quality in preschool centers, we began work on an extension to the ECERS-R that aimed to be sensitive to the kinds of learning opportunities the research literature described as "enhancing" or "supporting." Thus, the ECERS-E was developed to be used alongside the ECERS-R (see http://eppe.ioe.ac.uk), whose scales and indicators were based on the much-respected "Developmentally Appropriate Practice" (DAP) described in the 1980s by Bredekamp and Copple (1997). DAP had spelled out the kind of practice that would support a very broad array of developmental domains in children. However, the English curriculum (QCA, 2000) was based on more recent research literature, especially new literature on "emerging" development in literacy, numeracy, science, and the role of diversity and culture, particularly on the ways in which adults support learning in young children (see DfES, 2007a; Evangelou et al., 2009).

Behind the structure of the ECERS-E is the rich literature on the kinds of learning opportunities that underpin cognitive development in young children, especially those involving interactions with adults. Throughout the ECERS-E are items and indicators inspired by research on ways that adults "scaffold" learning in young children (Rogoff & Lave, 1999; Wood, Bruner, & Ross, 1976), "extend" their language (Snow, 2006), support "sustained shared thinking" (Siraj-Blatchford et al., 2003), and cater to their individual needs. The literature led to a conceptualization of the support for learning and development that could be assessed though an observation rating scale.

Although the ECERS-R assesses the environment for "emerging" academic skills, the items and indicators are not described in sufficient depth to accommodate the detailed English preschool curriculum. For example, the quality of educational provision that supports the emergence of literacy, numeracy, and cultural and scientific thinking was not sufficiently detailed for the ambitious English curriculum, so each of these areas was given a separate subscale in the ECERS-E. The fourth subscale, "Diversity," was devised to assess the extent to which staff differentiated the three cognitive domains when implemented with respect to children of different genders, cultural/ethnic groups, and varying levels of ability. Despite differences in England's national preschool curriculum and the many curricula adopted by U.S. states, we believe that the ECERS-E assesses fundamental conditions for fostering children's cognitive development that transcend different countries' prescribed curricular provisions. Not having the ECERS-E tied to a specific curriculum is one of the strengths of the instrument, which makes it particularly appropriate for use in the United States and other countries.

The English *Early Years Foundation Stage Curriculum* (DfES, 2007a) also includes three other curricular domains of development: creative; physical; and personal, social, and emotional. These affective domains are thoroughly assessed by the ECERS-R and so are not included in the ECERS-E. From the very beginning the extension to the ECERS-R was intended to supplement it, not replace it (Soucacou & Sylva, 2010).

Consider one of the ECERS-E subscales. The following shows how it is based on sound research literature. The model of literacy development on which the "Literacy" subscale is based stems from Whitehurst and Lonigan (1998), who defined "emergent literacy" as the "skills, knowledge and attitudes that are presumed to be developmental precursors to reading and writing." Other researchers (Sulzby & Teale, 1991) have similar conceptions. Included in the many studies of emergent literacy is the importance of the *social environment,* including shared book reading and discussion about the text. In this view of emergent literacy, the eventual acquisition of reading is conceptualized as a developmental continuum, with origins early in the life of the child. This is in sharp contrast to considering reading as an all-or-none phenomenon that begins when children start school (Storch & Whitehurst, 2001; Whitehurst & Lonigan, 1998). Within the concept of emergent literacy, there is no clear demarcation between reading and pre-reading, with literacy related behaviors "emerging" well before entry to school and supported by many different kinds of interactions and texts. Thus, there is a continuum of literacy acquisition that includes all of the preschool period. The origins of the skills needed to read and write can be found in the interactions that take place in the home and in the preschool setting, especially in children's exposure to interactions with print within social contexts (for example, book reading or eye-catching words used in the child's immediate environment, such as on packaging or signs naming well-known businesses like McDonald's).

Emergent literacy includes children's conceptual knowledge about literacy as well as their procedural knowledge about reading and writing. Here, children's "pretend reading" and "invented writing" are important precursors to reading and the formal writing that take place later in the school years (Mason & Stewart, 1990; Senechal, Lefevre, Smith-Chant, & Colton, 2001). We had a vast literature on emergent literacy (less so on emergent numeracy, science, and understanding of difference and diversity) to aid us in constructing indicators for an environment that would support children's emergent literacy in the preschool setting.

Because of the above, we believe the ECERS-E transcends national curricula and has proven to work particularly well in the U.S. context. Although developed in the United Kingdom with a specific curriculum in mind, the underlying principles on which the scales are based sit within what is universally considered good practice for young children. The scales have been and will continue to be used successfully in the United States and the rest of world in situations where considerations of quality matter.

Understanding the Nature of the ECERS-E

The ECERS-E was published in 2003 as a "research edition." Our goal was to share supplementary material providing more fine-grained assessment of curricula and pedagogy in early childhood settings, with researchers in the United Kingdom and elsewhere, particularly in the United States, who were using ECERS-R.

When the ECERS-E was originally developed, it was being used by a team of researchers who knew the scale and its aims very well. Additional notes and clarifications were not provided for the items and indicators because the people using it understood the intent and how each should be interpreted. However, now that the scales are being more widely used, it has become necessary to provide additional notes and clarification to support users in applying the scale consistently and appropriately. As questions were received by us and by others training on the scales, additional clarifications were developed for each item in response to those queries. These notes have improved the consistent use of the scale, but it is important to understand that the notes are intended to support the professional judgment of observers, not to constrain them.

ECERS-E and Assessing Pedagogy: The "Spirit" of the Scale

Although the individual subscales bear the titles of curricular areas such as "Mathematics," the quality ratings within each item are tuned to pedagogy and resources, as well as to curriculum. Across the four subscales, each item is scored with reference to pedagogy, resources, and the setting's organization. Discrete indicators usually focus on one of these at a time.

Settings that score well on the ECERS-E will be those in which there is a balance of child- and adult-initiated activity and a good deal of "sustained shared thinking" based on a pedagogy of co-construction (Siraj-Blatchford et al., 2002). Credit is also given across all four subscales for evidence of planning and child assessment, according to children's individual needs and interests.

- Many of the items are scored 3 if the pedagogy seems "accidental" or lacks coherence.
- A score of 5 is given if the setting shows evidence of adult guidance balanced with child play and/or exploration.
- A score of 7 is reserved for pedagogy in which adult and child both contribute to the construction of shared meanings, knowledge, and skills.

Materials are scored in the same way, with a 3 given for limited although appropriate materials, a 5 given to a wider array of materials, and a 7 reserved for materials suited to active use by children of differing capabilities, cultural backgrounds, and interests.

Cautions in Use

The ECERS-R was developed as a tool for research, but also as an instrument to guide practice. In contrast, the ECERS-E was originally developed solely for research purposes. It was created as part of the EPPE project as an extension to the ECERS-R in order to ensure greater depth and rigor in certain areas, specifically in the domains aimed at fostering children's emerging literacy, numeracy, and scientific thinking. The ECERS-E is now also widely used as a tool for quality improvement and can offer valuable guidance in this regard. However, it is important for two reasons to remember the context in which the scale was developed:

1. The ECERS-E was designed as an extension to the ECERS-R, rather than as a stand-alone tool, and it is important that it is not presented or used as such. It focuses on certain aspects of curricular provision (i.e., literacy, math, science/environment, and diversity) while not addressing others (e.g., creativity, personal, social education, ICT). The fact that these other aspects are not addressed by the ECERS-E does not mean that they are less important than literacy, math, or science, but simply reflect that they were not the focus of the EPPE project. Presenting the ECERS-E as a stand-alone tool may give the impression that the areas it addresses are more important than other areas, and this is not our intention. When used alongside the ECERS-R as intended, ECERS-E adds greater depth to certain areas.

2. The ECERS-E was designed to assess quality, rather than as a specific professional development tool. Accordingly, the items of the scale do not provide a comprehensive series of steps to work through in developing quality within a particular area. Rather, they contain a series of "indicators" of quality at each level. For example, the indicators representing 7 (excellent) within the item "Emergent writing/mark making" are examples of the kinds of experiences one might see in excellent settings. However, they do not necessarily include every single requirement one would expect in a high-quality environment. It is important that settings do not adopt a "checklist" approach and seek to address the requirements listed in the ECERS-E to the exclusion of

other improvements simply because they are the ones that are listed. This would not be in the spirit of the scales.

3. As stated above, the ECERS cannot cover all aspects of preschool practice; neither does it provide universal coverage within its subscales. Settings which score a 7 across the board will still need to consider their developmental needs. There is always room for improvement.

4. Settings that have been successful in using ECERS-R and ECERS-E for critical evaluation of their own curricula, provisions, and practices have found them particularly useful as tools to open up debate among their practitioners about what constitutes "quality." Having this debate before embarking on the administration of the scales can lead to a more supportive culture in which to make changes and a deeper understanding of quality. During training sessions practitioners have often commented on how they value working "with the scales" as opposed to having "ECERS done to them" (see later section on "Using ECERS as a Self-Assessment and Improvement Tool").

Terminology

It is useful to note that the broad headings of Literacy, Mathematics, Science and the Environment, and Diversity are referred to as *subscales*. Each subheading within a subscale is referred to as an *item* and each text block within the item is referred to as an *indicator*. For example:

Subscale = Literacy
Item = Print in the Environment
Indicator 1.1 = No labeled pictures are visible to the children

Throughout the scale, the word "staff" is used as a generic term to cover all adults who work regularly with children in the setting being observed. These could include volunteers, trainees, or students, as well as paid staff members.

When resources are described as "accessible," it means that children can get to them unassisted and for a substantial part of the day.

Before Using the Scales

Before using the ECERS-E scale either as a self-assessment tool (see next section) or as a research instrument, users are strongly recommended to familiarize themselves with the ECERS-R scale. Teachers College Press has produced a range of materials to accompany the ECERS-R for training purposes. These include video exercises and advice on making judgments. These materials can be used for both group and self-instruction. After viewing the training package, users will need to conduct several trial observations in order to familiarize themselves with the content of the items included in the scale. This cannot be done in a single observation (see Cryer, Harms, & Riley, 2003; Harms & Cryer, 2006).

Using the scales demands a high degree of understanding about not only the content of the scales but also with regard to making sense of what is being observed. In many cases information to complete the scales cannot be readily observed and the user will need to question the staff sensitively about their practices. Any user, therefore, needs to be familiar with the content of the scales and also must be confident in probing for additional information. Having a background grounded in early-years practice, including a good understanding of appropriate early-years practice and child development, will be an asset in making judgments in early-years settings.

Before using the scales, users should note that it is *strongly* recommended that they have external training and that their judgments are assessed for reliability. Being "reliable" on the scale means you have been assessed by an independent observer or inter-rater (trained to a specific standard) and that your scores concur with their independent "gold standard." This validates the results of an assessment. Inter-rater reliability is the extent to which two people observing the same environment produce similar scores. The inter-rater is the external observer. Training is available for those wishing to use the scales by contacting the Frank Porter Graham Child Development Institute at the University of North Carolina, Chapel Hill or A+ Education Ltd. (www.aplus-education.co.uk).

Using the ECERS-E

Preparing for the Observation

The ECERS-R had been designed to focus on activities and behaviors that occur frequently and are thus easy to score during a half-day's visit. One of the biggest problems with designing items for specific curricular areas like mathematics was to find ways to score an item where the essential information might not be observed in a one-day visit. Many math and science activities do not take place daily, so the developers of the ECERS-E encountered a sampling problem. How could the scorer "give credit" for activities that were part of the weekly plan but not seen on the day of the visit? This is why, in the science and math subscales, we offer a choice of items for rating. The ECERS-R did not rely heavily on a review of documents or the planning sheets of the staff. The newer ECERS-E, however, had to obtain information by consulting *planning* documents (P), by examining children's *records* for evidence about practices (R), and by examining *displays* around the room, e.g., photographs of yesterday's science activities (D). This was made possible by the emphasis in U.K. practice on planning for the year, the term, the week, and the day, which made the job of the observer much easier than it would have been in countries with a less-developed planning tradition (see the following section on "Use of Supplementary [Non-Observation] Evidence").

The following should be kept in mind when preparing for the observation:

- As with the other Environment Rating Scales, the ECERS-E is designed to be used with one group of children at a time. All areas to which the group of children have access should be observed.
- Sufficient time should be allocated to conduct the observations. At least 3 or 4 hours should be set aside to complete the ECERS-E. However, more time may be needed to see the range of activities assessed and to gain an accurate picture of the setting's provisions. It is recommended that you observe for *at least 6 hours* (for example, from 9:00 am to 3:00 pm).
- If you are using both the ECERS-R and the ECERS-E, you may want to complete the ECERS-R after the first few hours (the authors of the ECERS-R recommend an observation time of 3 to 4 hours) and then continue observing to gather more evidence for the ECERS-E.
- You will need some time at the end of the observation to talk with a member of staff and ask any additional questions. This should be at a time when the staff member is free from childcare responsibilities. You

will also need to have access to paperwork, such as planning documents and child observations/records, and you may need to allow extra time to ask questions about these if necessary. It is advisable to let the setting know before your visit that you will be asking to see documentation. Allow sufficient time for staff to get this for you.
- Before beginning the observation, ensure you have completed as much of the identifying information as possible: name of the center, age group observed, etc.
- Spend some time before the observation familiarizing yourself with the center and its geography. It is a good idea to find out from the staff what activities are planned for the period of the observation.
- Make sure that you are clear about the definitions of the terms used throughout the scale. For example, "a few" (Print in the environment, 3.1) suggests a limited number, probably no more than five, however "many" (same item, 5.1) suggests more than five. Clear distinctions (% value) should be made between "few," "some," "many," "variety," "most," "sometimes" and agreed by the observer and inter-rater. In this context, "easily accessible" pertaining to books and literacy areas means that children can reach and use materials easily, not necessarily that every child has to have access to all materials at all times. The term "staff" refers to all adults who have direct contact with children.

Using the ECERS-R and ECERS-E Together

- It is intended that the ECERS-E and ECERS-R be applied together on the same day. The ECERS-E requires a full day of observation because some of the activities and resources it assesses may appear infrequently. For example, a small-group activity on growing and nurturing seeds (Item 10: Natural materials) might take place in the afternoon when one of the parents is available to come into the center to work with the children. Therefore, observing this particular center only in the morning might lead to a lower score than is appropriate.
- One well-trained observer can do all of the observing, interviewing, and note-taking required in the two instruments during a single-day visit—although he or she will be working at a very intensive pace. If the center is only open for half a day, then two back-to-back sessions should be arranged. The observer is advised to arrive early to witness the arrival of children and parents and to spend the morning making

observation and taking notes. At the end of the part-day/session, there needs to be a "stock-taking" of the items and indicators that can be scored clearly and those for which further information will be needed. The lunchtime break is a good time to set up an interview with an informed staff member. It is during this interview that records on individual children and on planning can be sought. The second part-day session should be spent in confirming scores made during the morning and in finalizing those items/indicators that have not yet been resolved. It is ideal if a staff member can be available at the end of the two-part observation to answer any last-minute questions or to point out displays, planning documents, or resources about which there are questions.

Conducting the Observation

1. The items do not have to be completed in the order in which they appear in the book. If a cooking activity is taking place you may decide to score this immediately and then come back to other items later. Some items may be scored more easily than others.
2. Only score an item after you have allowed sufficient time to make a reasoned judgment. This is particularly important for items that demand observations of adult/child or child/child interactions. You need to be sure that what you are observing is representative of the setting's practices as a whole.
3. Take care not to interrupt the activities being observed. The observer should be like a "fly on the wall" and should avoid interacting with the children or staff. It is important to be as unobtrusive as possible and to remain neutral in your actions, expressions, and replies to questions.
4. If you are unsure about something, make detailed notes on your scoring sheet and ensure they are clear enough for you to follow when you come back to them at the end of the observation. Then discuss them with a "critical friend" in order to make a sound judgment. This is particularly important if you are using the scales for self-evaluation and plan to give feedback to others on your observations.
5. Make sure you score **all** of the items at the time of the observation. It is very difficult to record scores away from the setting.
6. A new score sheet should be used for each observation (permission is granted to photocopy score sheets only) and you should take care that the scoring is both legible and photocopiable. It is recommended that you use a pencil and have an eraser with you to amend scoring as you work.

Scoring the Scales

Scoring should only be attempted once the observer is familiar with the scale. Read the items carefully. It is essential that judgments are made exactly in accordance with the instructions given.

1. Scores must reflect the observed practice and not some future plan the staff may have told you about.
2. The scale measures quality on a range from 1 to 7, with 1 = inadequate, 3 = minimal, 5 = good, and 7 = excellent.
3. The observation should always start with 1 and be worked though systematically.
4. A rating of 1 must be given if **any** indicator in section 1 is scored YES.
5. A rating of 2 is given when **all** indicators under 1 are scored NO and at least half of the indicators under 3 are scored YES.
6. A rating of 3 is given when **all** indicators under 1 scored NO and all indictors under 3 are scored YES.
7. A rating of 4 is given when **all** indicators under 3 are met and at least half of the indicators under 5 are scored YES.
8. A rating of 5 is given when **all** indicators under 5 are scored YES.
9. A rating of 6 is given when **all** indicators under 5 are met and at least half of the indicators under 7 are scored YES.
10. A rating of 7 is given when **all** indicators under 7 are scored YES.
11. A score of NA (Not Applicable) may only be given for entire items where there are options (e.g., 9a: Shape or 9b: Sorting, matching and comparing). These items have an NA option on the score sheet.
12. To calculate average subscale scores, add up the scores for each item in the subscale and divide by the number of items scored. The total mean scale score is the sum of all item scores for the entire scale, divided by the number of items scored.

Note: These administrative guidelines are based on the ECERS-R. We are grateful to the Chapel Hill Team for their assistance in developing these.

Optional Scoring Systems

Unlike the ECERS-R, the ECERS-E has optional items. The ECERS-E focuses on opportunities to provide learning experiences; there may, however, be activities not evident during the observations that nevertheless cover important aspects of the curriculum. Before choosing which of the optional items to assess, look carefully at the range of activities offered during the observation period to see which item has the most evidence at-hand for scoring. If you are in doubt, score all of the items, including the optional ones, and then make a judgment on which optional item most accurately reflects the children's overall experiences in that curriculum area.

Some items in the math and science subscales are optional. The first two math items are always scored. The observer should then select either "Shape" or "Sorting, matching and comparing."

The first two science items are always scored. The observer should then select either "Non-living," "Living processes" or "Food preparation."

The idea behind the optional system is to make the observation manageable for all settings. The ECERS-E assesses complex pedagogical interactions, and it would be impossible (or unrealistic) to expect to see all of the behaviors and activities listed in the scale during a single observation. The optional-item system allows us to give credit for what is most evident on the observation day.

For example, the three optional science items assess the same concepts (e.g., where staff are encouraging children to use different senses to explore and talk about their experiences) but from different domains of science: "Non-living," "Living processes," and "Food preparation." Usually we would not decide which of these areas to score until later in the observation. It is good practice to gather evidence for all optional items and then decide at the end which can be scored the highest. For example, if you see a baking activity you might have gathered more evidence for "Food preparation" than for the other options. In this case, you would complete the scoring for this item and cross through the other two optional science items. In this way, you can give the setting credit for their best practice on the day.

In terms of scoring, you would always submit three item scores for "Science"—Items 1 and 2, and then whichever of the optional items you choose. If you are a practitioner using the scales in a more developmental way (e.g., over time to support improvements in practice), then you might want to use all of the optional items.

Use of Supplementary (Non-Observation) Evidence

Using Evidence from Planning Documents

The late 1990s saw a major shift in educational policy relating to early years childcare and education in the U.K. A series of influential reports recommended expanding early education and a more integrated approach to services for young children and their parents (DES, 1990; Ball, 1994; Audit Commission, 1996). The benefits of early education were also supported by research evidence (Sylva et al., 2004).

This led firstly to the development of a set of 'guidelines' (QCA, 2000) which set out a framework for the education of young children and then later statutory standards for the 'learning, development and care for children from birth to five' (DfES, 2007a). The statutory framework makes clear that children must be engaged in educational programs which cover 6 main areas of learning and development: Personal, social and emotional development, Communication, language and literacy, Problem solving, reasoning and numeracy, Knowledge and understanding of the world, Physical development and Creative development. Not only are practitioners expected to provide opportunities for children to flourish in these areas but they must also monitor children's learning and progress. This has to be accomplished by statutory assessment arrangements which state that 'ongoing assessment is an integral part of the learning and development process' (DfES, 2007b, p16). To this end there has been an increased emphasis, in the U.K., on not only monitoring children's development and progress but also providing evidence to demonstrate that the programs of activities provided by a setting is matched to the developmental needs of their children.

Providing evidence through explicit plans has become normal practice in the U.K. and whilst the quality of plans may vary from setting to setting, all settings have a statutory obligation to provide plans for inspection purposes and individual profiles of children for reporting to parents.

The types of plans most evident in the U.K. are those which deal with long, medium and short term time periods. Long term plans could cover up to a full year and would show broadly how the 6 areas of development would be addressed. This provides an overview, with the medium term (usually broken up in 6 week blocks) providing more detail on the activities which will be used to promote learning. The short term plans (weekly or daily) would then provide the more fine grained detail of the specific activities individual (or groups) of children will be engaged in. Planning in the U.K. is distinguished by the level of detail which goes beyond a posted schedule of daily activities and it is usually based upon observations of individual or groups of children's learning and their interests. While a posted schedule may also be used to provide parents with an "at a glance" look at what their children may be doing over a session, it would be based on a much more detailed written plan produced by staff.

Plans in the U.K. usually not only contain details of activities but would also require these to be evaluated. Here the practitioner would clearly identify the learning objectives of the activity and then comment on whether or not this was met. The practitioner would usually reflect on what went well, what didn't go well and what would need to be changed in subsequent activities. In addition to evaluating the plan, extensive comments would usually be kept on the individual children whilst they were engaged in activities in order to satisfy the evidence required to complete each child's individual Early Years Foundation Stage Profile (QCA/DfES, 2003). The Early Years Foundation Stage Profile is a document which by law all centers must complete in order to monitor a child's developmental progress. As a child moved through the U.K.'s education system the Profile 'tracks' their achievements and indicates what areas of development have been achieved and what remains to be developed. The Profile is also used extensively to report to parents on their child's accomplishments.

Caution When Using Planning as Evidence

When conducting an ECERS-E observation in the United Kingdom, it has become common practice to use planning documents as additional evidence to support the rater's judgments, since they contain rich information about children's experiences. However, we would urge extreme caution when using planning evidence—using it alone, without observational verification, could lead to poor judgments.

One of the biggest challenges in considering planning is the extent to which the written plan may or may not have been carried out. Some centers may adhere rigidly to plans, while in other centers plans may be nothing more than paper exercises. Some settings may vary plans according to the needs and interests of the children; others, for the convenience of staff. The rater therefore has to have some confidence in the capacity of the center to produce meaningful plans. When plans contain no evaluation or commentary or reference to what children actually did (as opposed to what they were meant to do), they should be treated with caution. Good planning may legitimately be changed during implementation but these changes should be clearly documented and the rater should be able to follow a plan through from conception to delivery. Similarly, planning in and of itself cannot give clues about the quality of the experience. However, good plans, when they are evaluated well , can give significant insight into the quality of the experience.

The ECERS-R was designed to focus on activities and behaviors that occur frequently and are thus easy to score during a half-day's visit. The biggest problem with designing items for specific curricular areas, such as mathematics, was to find ways to score an item where the essential information might not be observed in a 1-day visit. Many math and science activities do not take place daily, so we encountered a sampling problem. How could the scorer "give credit" for activities that were part of the weekly plan but were not seen on the day of the visit? So, unlike the ECERS-R, observers using the new ECERS-E have to obtain information by consulting *planning* documents (P), by examining children's *records* for evidence about practices (R), and by examining *displays* around the room, e.g., photographs of yesterday's science activities (D). Unlike countries with a less-developed planning tradition, this is easier in the United Kingdom because of the emphasis in English practice on planning for the year, the term, the week, and the day. The ECERS-R scales identify where planning can be used as evidence, but again we urge caution in an over-reliance on this when making observational judgments.

Since the ECERS-E is an observational scale, the majority of activities and behaviors will need to be observed to give credit. In some cases, supplementary evidence can be used (e.g., display or children's records/portfolios). Where it is appropriate to supplement observation with evidence from other sources, individual items are marked as follows:

P—evidence from *planning* acceptable

D—evidence from *displays*/photographic records acceptable

R—evidence from children's *records* acceptable (includes children's portfolios or folders of completed work)

Q—evidence from *questioning* acceptable.

Note: These letters are also marked on the score sheet next to the relevant indicators. When scoring, these letters can be circled to show which source of evidence was used.

Throughout the scale, indicators for which evidence other than observations can be used are marked accordingly (using P, D, R, and/or Q). A small number of these relate specifically to planning and/or records, and *require* evidence to be present in these forms. For example, the following indicator from the Science subscale requires that the introduction of scientific concepts needs to be planned for. In this case, planning evidence is *required*:

5.1 Staff often plan and introduce appropriate scientific concepts (Ex. how materials change, magnetism, sinkers and floaters) and children handle materials.* P, D, R

However, for most of the items that allow evidence from supplementary sources, these additional sources should only be sought when "observable" examples are lacking. Observation always provides the best evidence, since there is no way of knowing how well a particular activity was carried out when using display or records (or, in the case of planning evidence, whether the activity was carried out at all). For example, in the following indicator from the Science subscale, credit can be given if this is observed on the day. But if no examples are directly observed, then evidence from planning and/or display may be used instead:

5.1 Natural materials are used beyond decoration to illustrate specific concepts (Ex. planting seeds or bulbs to demonstrate growth).* P, D

Do not give credit for activities shown in the planning where your observations on the day do not support the planning evidence.

In some cases, evidence from planning, records and/or display can only be used as *supporting* evidence and a particular activity must also be observed to give credit. **In these cases, the P, D, and R are shown in parentheses:**

7.1 Children are encouraged to identify and explore a range of natural phenomena in their environment outside the center and talk about/ describe them.* (P), (D)

The notes for this indicator make it clear that at least one discussion relating to nature/natural materials should be observed. Planning or display evidence can then be used as supporting evidence as to whether children experience a range of natural phenomena.

How Much Evidence to Review?

When using the ECERS-E for assessment we suggest that the observer reviews a sample of paper-based evidence:

- Long-, medium-, and short-term planning for progress (or at least the most recent plans, possibly covering the previous 6 weeks if these are fairly typical)*;
- Records (e.g., learning stories, portfolios of children's work) kept on three children. If possible, records should show a range of ages/stages—for example, one child who is ahead of the group in one or more areas, a child in the mid-range, and a child who struggles in one or more areas;
- Paperwork relating to at least one child with additional or special needs (recorded in a child's Individual Education Plan if applicable);

- The current displays in the room (e.g., photos of recent activities, books prepared for parents to show recent activities carried out by the group, display boards of children's work). As a general guide, if display is used as evidence, it should be no more than 6–8 weeks old.

Note: It is also advisable to ask a member of staff to talk you through the planning and record-keeping process.

*Some evidence of planning for progress should be available for approximately the past 6 typical weeks. It is recognized that short-term planning will be in response to children's interests and needs and cannot be completed much in advance, whereas medium-term planning around, for example, continuous curriculum areas, possible themes, and seasonal enhancements should reflect the work of the setting and be available. Long-term objectives and both short-term and longitudinal planning should be documented in some way.

Throughout the scale, where evidence from planning, records, or display is acceptable, guidelines are suggested as to how many examples should be seen within the evidence reviewed. But these guidelines are not hard and fast, as every setting plans and records evidence in a different way. Observers should also use their judgment about whether a particular activity or concept is adequately provided for. Where the ECERS-E is being used in a more developmental way (e.g., by a staff team over time), it is useful to consider more than a 6-week period of planning, and to review children's records more comprehensively.

Planning in England

Probably what most distinguishes England from the United States and other international contexts is the extent to which activities and experiences are explicitly planned in relation to children's interests and the national curriculum. In addition, there are statutory regulations regarding recording children's attainments and progress, which includes systematically recording children's achievements to monitor their progress. The introduction of a national set of curricular guidelines (QCA, 2000) for early-years practitioners was followed by a set of statutory obligations to ensure that a formal record of children's achievements is kept (QCA & DfES, 2003). This record of an individual child's achievement must ensure that all staff members working with the child:

- understand the child's stage of development (summative records),
- can plan appropriate activities based on the child's needs (formative records) and,
- pass on important information accurately to other practitioners and parents.

In order to help practitioners manage this process, a specific government agency was set up. The National Strategies provided face-to-face training and online support to help all those working with young children to translate national policy into everyday practice. All those working with young children have to ensure that the learning environment is well-planned and well-organized and challenges children in their development. The "learning environment" is defined in terms of resources, organization, adult role, and any experiences that can potentially be harnessed to stimulate children's thinking and development. This includes not only explicitly planned activities, but also routine tasks such as the start/end of sessions, story time, hand-washing, tidying-up, and greetings and departures. Good planning in the English context includes the offer of a broad and balanced curriculum alongside learning opportunities for *all* children in keeping with their interests, abilities, culture, and gender. The planning should include long-, medium-, and short-term plans. While government agencies give advice on planning, there is no one framework that everyone must use. Individual centers are able to develop their own systems for planning, provided they satisfy the national guideline on what should be recorded.

The next section gives two examples of planning to illustrate the kind of evidence ECERS raters in the United Kingdom seek when scoring. Example 1 comes from the U.K.'s National Strategies (http://nationalstrategies.standards. dcsf.gov.uk/earlyyears) which provides practitioners with a range of materials to help them plan. Information on the National Strategies website is free to download, but Crown Copyright cannot be reproduced without a licence from the U.K. Government. We are grateful to the National Strategies for allowing permission to reproduce this Crown Copyrighted material under License No C2010000736 in Example 1. We are grateful to Sandra Mathers and Faye Linskey of A+ Education Ltd. (www.aplus-eduction.co.uk) for providing the material in Example 2.

Every early-years practitioner (or key worker) has to produce long-, medium-, and short-term plans for the children in their care. In larger centers this is often done as a group exercise, with practitioners sharing their expertise. Planning in England includes:

Long-Term Plans

The long-term plan would show the general topics to be covered for a whole year and how these link with the six key areas of development:

1. Personal, Social, and Emotional Development (PSED)
2. Communication, Language, and Literacy (CLL)
3. Creative Development (CD)
4. Physical Development (PD)
5. Knowledge and Understanding of the World (KUW)
6. Problem Solving, Reasoning, and Numeracy (PSRN)

A long-term plan may be quite general but must provide a basis for developing the medium-term plan. Long-term plans should be clearly displayed for parents.

Medium-Term Plans

These plans outline in more detail the overall program for usually up to 6 weeks and give more detail on individual activities and areas of learning. As research has shown (Siraj-Blatchford et al., 2002) the most effective settings have a balance between child-led and adult-initiated activities. Practitioners are encouraged to achieve a balance between activities planned in response to individual children's interests and those planned to ensure a balance across the curriculum.

Short-Term Plans

It is in short-term planning that skillful practitioners manage to meld individual children's interests and needs together to ensure that, during a given period, all children have the opportunity to develop their skills in a context that is meaningful to them. At the heart of the assessment program is the individual child. Practitioners are encouraged through systematic observations and discussions to identify a child's individual strengths, weaknesses, and interests, and then to link these to the six key areas of development.

Note the abbreviations used in this list: they are used extensively in the planning sheets presented throughout this section.

Example 1

In the example at the top of the next column, Child C's key worker has identified her preoccupation with tractors and has translated this into an "Individual Plan" to see how this might help Child C develop across the 6 key areas. Here the key worker has identified a number of activities that might motivate Child C and has

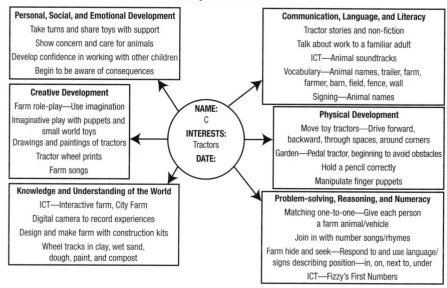

Example: Individual Plan

created an individual learning plan for this child. In addition, the key worker would talk with Child C's parent to see if this interest is sustained at home and suggest ways the parents might support her learning through her interest in tractors. This information is added to Child C's Individual Plan as follows:

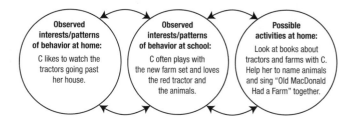

This detailed planning would be done for **every child.** Only after this information is gathered would a short-term weekly plan be drawn up that identifies activities that would cover the needs of individuals, groups, or the majority of children. The next stage of the plan is to show activities for a week. The plan below shows activities which are *adult initiated*. Note that items in **bold are activities planned in response to the children's interests** and activities not in bold are those planned to ensure a balance across the curriculum. Child C's interests are included explicitly in adult-initiated activities on Tuesday (printing), Wednesday (story), and Thursday (soundtracks).

Date:	Monday	Tuesday	Wednesday	Thursday	Friday
Adult-Initiated Special Activity or New Provision	Mix paints **Tuff Spot, dogs, and "biscuits"**	Spread crackers, cut and taste avocado, tomato, peppers and cucumber **Tractor wheel printing**	**Digging the vegetable patch Story role-play**	Music **CD Player—animal soundtracks**	Autumn weather walk Croissants and hot chocolate

Next, ongoing continuous (daily) activities (not adult-initiated but laid out on tables) are also planned with the interests of children in mind:

Continuous Provision					
Malleable materials	Dough, activity set	Clay, tools, and sponges	Cornflour and water	Dough and cutters	Dry paints
Sand	**Free choice**	Dinosaurs	**Tractors and diggers**	Wheels	Containers with holes
Water	Boats and people	Green water and containers	Bubbles	Recycled materials	**Free choice**
Design and Tech Area	Building bricks	**Farm and dolls' house**	**Free choice**	Train set	Wooden bricks
Information Technology	Tizzy's Busy Week	**Fizzy's Numbers**	Musical leaps and bounds	2Simple paint	Alphabet soup
Puzzles, toys, games	**Quack Quack game**	People puzzles	Books and toys	**Cobble Road maths game**	Magnetic letters
Stories and group times	**"Little Farmer Joe" & number rhymes**	**"Webster J Duck" & number rhymes**	**"And the Good Brown Earth" & number rhymes**	**"Handa's Hen" & music, number rhymes**	**"Roaring Rockets" & number rhymes**
Food and drinks	Milk, apples	Milk, crackers, tomato, avocado, cucumber	Milk, carrots	Milk, bananas	Hot chocolate/croissants
Garden (activities vary according to the weather)	Spades, buckets, seeds, and dibbers Large sand tray	Large water equipment, aqua play	**Push-along tractors** Rakes, spades	**Push-along tractors and toys**	Wheelbarrows, rakes, buckets, sweeping brushes

Again the **bold** typeface indicates activities that will specifically appeal to the identified interests of named children. Child C's interests are being catered to in the activities that include tractors and the emphasis during story time on farms. The next stage of planning is to take these ongoing continuous activities and add some additional depth, so it is clear what learning concepts are being addressed. In the example below, two ongoing continuous activities, Food and Drinks, have been expanded to show in more detail the specific learning content:

A.M.	Monday	Tuesday	Wednesday	Thursday	Friday
Milk and snack	Work together to prepare milk and fruit • Begin to work with another child with support *Signs—help, give*	Work together to prepare milk and fruit • Begin to recite numbers in order Count objects accurately **(Child K, J)**	Work together to prepare milk and fruit • To count objects accurately • To give explanations	Work together to prepare milk and fruit • Use mathematical knowledge to begin to solve problems	Make groups of cartons • Begin to say when two groups have the same number
Story	*Little Farmer Joe* • To begin to name feelings **(Child H, A: express own feelings)** *Signs—happy, sad*	*Webster J. Duck* • To distinguish sounds **(Child J, C: link sound to animal)** • To notice detail in pictures *Signs—animal names*	*And The Good Brown Earth* • To make links with previous experiences • To talk about recent events **(Child A, N: with support)** *Signs—what, who*	*Handa's Hen* • Begin to be aware of people and cultures • Begin to count objects that cannot be moved **(Child M, E: recite numbers in order)**	*Roaring Rockets* • Begin to be aware of rhyming words **(Child J, H: join in with rhyme)** *Sign—listen*

This planning sheet shows in more detail what the learning focus is of each activity and highlights particular children who are to be the focus in these activities. So Child C is marked out for particular inclusion in Tuesday's story activity. Individual children's responses to child-initiated play can also be recorded by hand, written into a grid after a session:

Additional activities	Collage materials, Bears and cave	Paint, wheel on tractor	*Going on a Bear Hunt*, Musical instruments	Stepping stones	Boxes, pebbles, dinosaurs, sand
Observation	H—using collage materials to make a rocket to take home and show his Dad. K, J, and A—role-play with bears and caves.	C—wheel prints using ride-on tractor in garden and paint in tough spot. All joined in.	K, J, and C—role-play and singing with Bear Hunt book. C joined in musical instruments outside.	M and E—stepping stones in garden. K, J, and C—looking for bears in the wild area.	T—box collection, pebbles, and dinosaurs in sand.

Note our emphasis showing **Child C.**

Planning would also take place that relates specific activities to the 6 key areas of development, for instance, taking account of Child C's interest in tractors. This interest prompted an adult-initiated activity, "tractor wheel printing," to be included in our first weekly planning example. The practitioner, in her "Plan for Focused Activities," has identified how this activity relates to the 6 key areas of development as follow:

Date: Tuesday		
Task: Tractor wheel printing		
Areas covered by this activity: **Personal, Social, and Emotional Development (PSED)** **Creative Development (CD)** **Physical Development (PD)** **Problem Solving, Reasoning, and Numeracy (PSRN)**		Areas not covered: Communication, Language, and Literacy (CLL) Knowledge and Understanding of the World (KUW)
Objective	*Vocabulary/Questions*	*Area of learning*
To explore mark-making	Print, mark, pattern, round, curve, straight, same, different	Personal, social, and emotional development/Creative development
To notice similarities and differences	Are the patterns the same? How are they different?	Problem solving, reasoning, and numeracy
To be aware of pattern, size, shape		Problem solving, reasoning, and numeracy
To put on own apron		Physical development
Target children: Ro, N, Ja, M, C, Re, L		

All of the above plans, plus observations on individual children, would be used to monitor how children have engaged with the activities over a 1-week period. These would be used for daily discussion on children's progress and at the end of the week when members of staff get together and review the notes on individual children. From these observations, the next day's/week's planning would be developed.

Example 2

This example is taken from a nursery school and, again, the long-term planning feeds into the medium-term planning, which then guides short-term plans.

Long-Term

In this center the staff develop long-term plans together to ensure that their learning environment supports and challenges children's development across the six areas of learning.

The learning environment covers resources, organization, adult roles, and potential learning experiences, both indoors and out (often known in the United Kingdom as "continuous provision"). As part of their continuous provision, the staff team make sure that they always offer the following:

role-play area	construction area	mark-making/office area	math area
sand and water area	creative area	malleable materials area	music area
painting area	book area	ict area	food preparation area
physical activity area	science area		

These areas are always available for children to access independently, with a range of resources to support the six areas of learning.

Staff also think about and discuss daily routines as part of their long-term planning, and consider their potential in terms of opportunities for learning and development (for example, the beginning and end of sessions, including registration; handover time for children from parent/carers to key workers and vice versa; snack and meal times; hand-washing and toilet/diaper-changing routines; and tidy-up time). In this setting, the long-term planned provision offers a broad and balanced curriculum and learning opportunities for all children—and also provides the basis for medium- and short-term planning.

Medium-Term

From the long-term plan this center then produces a planning chart or list at the beginning of every semester (a block of approximately 3–4 months) as part of the medium-term planning. Ideas on the current themes/interests are mapped out, and Possible Lines of Development (PLODs) are listed, as shown below. Often the themes develop from the children's interests and are not necessarily set in advance by staff. For example, the travel and transport theme developed after staff noticed the children's interest in a nearby building site, complete with construction vehicles. The possibilities for the theme were discussed with the children and their ideas were recorded to feed into the PLODs.

Other events in the term are also listed, as are any other relevant notes, for example, specific children's interests that might inform the choice of activities. For this term the events are: Pancake Day, Easter, Holi, and a visit by local musicians.

Term: Spring	
Theme: Travel and Transport	
Starting point: several children had shown an interest in watching the diggers on a building site next door to the setting.	
Possible Lines of Development	
Modes of transport e.g. car, bus, boat, plane, tractor, lorry	Vaneena's Dad to visit to talk about being a pilot
Looking at cars in detail	Using large blocks to build a car
Creating number plates	Running cars down different gradients of slope
Making tax discs	Junk model vehicles
Create a building site in the sand area	Create a garage outdoors for role play
Diggers and other vehicles in the sand to encourage construction	Numbering vehicles/bikes/parking spaces in outdoor area
Walk to local garage	Collecting natural items from walk
Observational drawings of natural objects collected on walk	Visit to a car wash/make car wash as part of the garage
Making maps	Treasure maps
Make directions for finding treasure	Navigating an obstacle course
Small world resources (e.g. lego): garage, train track, vehicles, floor road map	Mini treasure hunt in the sand tray with maps

The plan also contain notes on particular children's interests:

- Sam's dad has a new car
- Ruth, Nadid, Luke, and David are particularly interested in the building site next door
- Katy's dad works in a local garage
- Harry comes to the center on his scooter
- Vaneena's dad is a pilot.

Short-Term

The short-term plan is developed from the medium-term plan. It involves planning in response to individual needs and interests and includes activities/experiences selected from the medium-term plan. Short-term planning is usually done on a daily or weekly basis and sets out the learning objectives, foci for observation and assessment, targets and support for individuals, resources, key vocabulary, staff responsibilities, and practical information (e.g., timings).

The staff use the following planning techniques:

- A weekly plan of adult-directed activities plus enhanced provision (as shown below). The "enhanced provision" are the resources added to the continuous provision areas in order to develop the theme or topic, or to respond to children's interests. Where an activity was developed from a child's interest or is thought to be particularly appropriate for a child, children's initials are noted on the plan in bold. The 6 areas of learning are also recorded so that staff can check that all areas are covered during the week. Staff plan together on a weekly basis, with some notes made every day. Fridays are left blank and planned during the week, informed by observations and by the children's interests. At the end of each week, notes on new Possible Lines of Development for the following week are recorded.
- Daily plans for adult-focused activities are also completed, usually based on an individual child's interest and related to the theme (an example follows).

Week Commencing: February 23rd (Bold text = particular children)

	MONDAY	TUESDAY	WEDNESDAY	THURSDAY	FRIDAY
Themed activity	Walk to local garage using maps made by the children PSED; CLL; KUW	Making pancakes for Shrove Tuesday PSED; CLL; KUW	Walk to local garage using maps made by the children PSED; CLL; KUW	Mini treasure hunt in the sand tray with maps CLL; PSRN; CD	
Planned adult-focus	Remote control car: manipulation and route planning CLL; KUW; PSED **RB, NT, SS, KL, AP, LP, DR**	⟶		⟶	
Focus group time	Introducing our own objects of interest PSED; CLL; KUW; CD	Circle time PSED; CLL; CD	Sharing items collected on our walk PSED; CLL; KUW; CD	Creating an interest table showing maps and treasure PSED; CLL; KUW; CD	
ENHANCED PROVISION					
CLL	Looking at a selection of maps CLL; KUW	Creating our own maps CLL; KUW	⟶		
PSRN/Maths	Color and shape puzzles PSED; PSRN; PD	Number puzzles PSED; PSRN; PD	Sorting shapes PSED; PSRN; PD	Matching shape and color game PSED; PSRN; PD	
KUW/Science	Microscope and slides PSED; KUW; PD	Slopes—tractors, lorries and cars PSED; KUW; PD **SG, GB**	Looking through magnifying glass at items found on walk PSED; CLL; KUW	Magnets and selection of items PSED; KUW; PD **PT, NN**	
ICT and Computers	See planned adult focus	⟶		⟶	
Sand/Water	Wet and dry sand CLL; PD; CD	Imaginary cooking with a tea set, pots and pans PSED; CLL; PD	Building sand castles using buckets + spades PSED; PSRN;KUW	Colored water, tubes and funnels PSED; PSRN; PD **HT, MG**	
Physical Activity	Blowing and chasing bubbles KUW; PD; CD **NT, PP, FY**	Balancing using small equipment—beanbags, balls and hoops PSED; PD **LP, SS, RB, MK**	Navigating an obstacle course PSED; PD	Dancing to fast and slow music PSED; PD; CD	
Creative Area	Creating junk model vehicles KUW; PD; CD, PSED	⟶		⟶	
Sensory Area	Play dough with cutters and rollers CLL; PD; CD	Wet and dry pasta KUW; PD; CD	Using the conveyor belt with molded play dough objects CLL; PD; CD	Discovering properties of cornflour CLL; PD; CD **GG, GB, PT, NT**	
Imaginative Play	Cars and road maps KUW; PD; CD **NT, SS, KL, AP, LP, DR**	Train track KUW; PD; CD	Cars and road maps plus garage set KUW; PD; CD	Airplanes and helicopters PSED; PD; CD **RB, NT, SS, KL**	
Role Play	Ticket office CLL; KUW; CD; PSED	⟶		⟶	
NOTES					
Notes on Children's Interests					
Evaluation and PLODs for Next Week (Theme & Other Events)					

19

The planned adult focus shown below developed as a result of a child's particular interest, but was also identified as appropriate and interesting for a number of other children. All children would have access to the activity, but the information about individuals helps staff to pick up on particular interests and needs. The evaluation section from the previous day's activity (the first day on which remote control cars were introduced) shows the observations staff took into account when planning the activity for Feb. 24th.

Evaluation Section from Previous Day (Feb. 23rd)

Evaluation
Majority able to manipulate the remote control car & move it forward, backward, turn, etc. Extend to following simple routes (use big maps). Fred, Heather, Kayla may need support and less complex routes. Ruth and Katy show good grasp—draw own maps?

Planned Adult Focus, Feb. 24th—Available from 10:00 am to Mid-Day and 2:00 pm to 4:00 pm

Observational evidence towards interest:		
Nadid had shown a keen interest in using the road map with toy cars. When his key person mentions this to his Mom she says he is getting a remote-control car for his birthday that coming weekend. Other possible interested children: Sam (often seen joining Nadid when playing with the cars), Katy (always eager to find out how things work)		
Activity	**Key vocabulary/questions**	**Children for whom this activity might support their individual learning priorities**
Learning to manipulate a remote-control car to follow a route to the shops.	Forward/backwards	
Adult role	Further away/nearer to	Full time: Ruth, Nadid, Sam, Katy
Show the children how to use the controls. Encourage children to take turns to practice moving the car along different routes to the shops.	Left/right	Part time: Alex C (am), Luke (am), David (pm)
	Can you make the car stop?	
	Can you make the car move forwards?	
Focus for observation	**Resources**	**Adapting the activity for individual children**
How to operate simple equipment (KUW)	Remote-control car	*Support:*
Show an interest in why things happen and how things work (KUW)	Materials/boxes to customize car	Follow less complex routes & adult support (Fred, Heather, Kayla)
To share and take turns (PSED)	Large sheets of paper with routes on (different levels of complexity)	*Challenges:*
To work as part of a group (PSED)	Large sheets of paper to draw new routes	Draw out new routes and instructions. Pair with children who need more support and teach them how to use the remote-control car (Katy, Ruth)
Evaluation—The majority of children able to manipulate the remote control to follow simple routes. Fred, Heather, Alex C. need more support. David, Andrew, and Nadid worked particularly well together, co-operating and taking turns—tomorrow, encourage to draw additional routes (also Ellen, Josh). Katy & Ruth to plan routes around the nursery (e.g., to the office)—showed an interest in trying this.		

(example adapted from Curriculum Guidance for the Foundation Stage)

Observing Children

The success of good child-centered planning rests on the observational skills of the practitioner. Through observing each child's (and groups of children's) achievements and interests, skilled practitioners are able to plan new activities or change the environment in ways that help children learn. In this setting, children's individual learning priorities are recorded each half-term on one large sheet of paper. Two priorities are listed for each child, one short-term and one longer-term.

Brief observations are recorded daily using post-it notes. Each week the team also selects four or five children for detailed observation (see example below). Each key person collects and files the observations of the children that are assigned to him or her. Each child also has a "Learning Journey" (a personal portfolio/file), in which staff members post photos of the child taking part in different activities and jot down notes on what the child learned from the experience. At the end of the week, staff members have a short catch-up with the parents, who have been asked to contribute their observations of the children at home. This sharing of information between home and school helps build a more detailed picture of each child's needs, interests, and learning styles, and helps staff to review the children's individual learning priorities.

At the end of each day, the team meets for about half an hour to evaluate the day's activities and discuss the observations they made on individual children. These evaluations are used as a starting point for planning the next day's activities. In the evaluation that follows, which is from the previous day, the practitioner records how individuals within the group coped with the activity, and outlines the next steps for one particular child so that this can be incorporated into future planning.

Date: Feb. 24th   **Activity:** Learning to manipulate a remote-control car to follow a route to the shops.

Child: David   **Staff member:** Anna

Observation: David easily mastered programming the remote-control car. He worked with Andrew and Nadid to negotiate routes. He was confident within the group, co-operated, and took turns. Afterwards, he described in detail what he had done.

Early Learning Goals (please mark ELGs relevant to child's individual learning priorities with *)
How to operate simple equipment (KUW)
To share and take turns (PSED)*
To work as part of a group (PSED)*
Use talk to organize, sequence and clarify thinking, ideas, feelings, and events (CLL)

Next steps for this child: Draw additional routes for remote-control car. Over next few weeks, provide additional opportunities for working with other children in pairs or small groups.

(example adapted from curriculum guidance for the Foundation Stage)

This document cannot cover all aspects of planning, but it is hoped that the two examples presented above illustrate how important observing children, planning for and from their experiences, and evaluating their learning journeys is accorded a high priority in England.

Using ECERS as a Self-Assessment and Improvement Tool

ECERS-R and ECERS-E can be used in settings not only for improving practice but also for providing evidence of

- self-evaluation,
- reflective practice, and
- development planning

at both the center level and the state/federal level.

Improvement at the Center Level

Since the publication of the United Kingdom's Effective Provision of Pre-School Education (EPPE) Technical Papers, which relate quality—as measured by ECERS-R and ECERS-E—with child cognitive and social/behavioral developmental outcomes for children aged 3–5, we have been inundated with requests for the ECERS-E (which was particularly predictive for cognitive outcomes—see Introduction), not only from within the United Kingdom but also from around the world. We have asked people what they wanted the scale for and most replied that they want to use it in their early childhood settings for self-assessment or as a research instrument.

We discussed, as a team, what it means for people to use the scales when they haven't been trained to do so. We are concerned about their use in settings where the general professional training of the staff may be limited. We are certain that, under such circumstances, critical but constructive support will be needed. We also worry about the lack of external validation or external moderation, which allows settings to rate themselves as good, excellent, or in need of further development but with no real comparative measure.

Because of these concerns we used the ECERS-R and ECERS-E as part of the 3-year-long Early Excellence Evaluation of two U.K. centers: Gamesley Early Excellence Center in Derbyshire and the Thomas Coram Early Excellence Center in London (Siraj-Blatchford, 2002a, 2002b). With the support of their heads and senior teachers, the centers used the ECERS-R and ECERS-E scales as a self-development tool.

All staff first received a full-day's training on the meaning of "quality," the culturally specific aspects and what we consider to be the universal aspects, such as treating children with respect or not harming or smacking children. The staff were introduced to the ECERS-R and the ECERS-E and were trained by a trained researcher/user of the scales, using the ECERS-R video and training guide produced by Teachers College Press (Harms & Cryer, 2006).

The staff were given time to compare and discuss their judgments and then asked to try two of the scales for themselves, working in pairs. In a follow-up half-day session, they reported back their findings, including their agreements and disagreements.

During the 3 years the staff regularly reported on their discussions and progress with the scales. They found it easier to begin by rating the less-threatening subscales, such as furnishings and display. From this they learned that the actual *discussions* generated the most useful outcomes. These discussions led them to agree on meanings for good practice. The staff recommended that each rater discuss their ratings (undertaken independently, but based on the same observations), and then immediately compare their ratings and discuss why their perceptions sometimes differed. As the staff developed in confidence in their ratings and discussions, they became more critical of their setting and their practices, and at times also more critical about some aspects of the scales. All of this was perceived as productive, as most of their observations led to positive actions. For instance, the Thomas Coram EEC, after rating their center on the "Language and Reasoning" subscale, decided to take the following action:

Within 6 months:

- to provide in-service training for all staff on extending children's conversations, focusing on developing the use of open-ended questions
- to establish listening areas in the rooms used by children aged 3–5.

Within 1 year:

- to order more dress-up clothes and to increase the range and quality of the clothes for sociodramatic play.

Similarly, after rating the ECERS-R subscale on Personal Care Routines at the Gamesley EEC, staff made a decision on the item "Greetings and Departures." Although the staff felt that greeting the parents and children at the nursery was well-organized, some were concerned because the departure in the afternoon meant that some children missed out on the important story session. The staff also felt that there was insufficient time to talk or share information with the parents.

"**All very rushed**, parents also have to hunt for their children, as each nursery officer went into a different room for small group/story time" (Lynn Kennington, Head teacher, Gamesley EEC).

There was intense discussion among the staff about how to improve departure time.

Action taken: The arrival and departure time for children who attended the center in the afternoon was changed. The session used to start at 12:45 pm and finish at 3:15 pm. Now, instead of going into small groups for story time, all the nursery groups join together for a large-group story. The staff, on a rotating basis, read the story, and the parents collected their children from this group. This helps parents know where they can find their children, and gives the nursery officers who are not reading the story time to share information with parents about their child. The result was that the story sessions were no longer interrupted and there were opportunities for staff and parents to discuss matters regarding their children.

Both these centers documented and discussed examples from the ECERS-R and ECERS-E. They agreed on certain actions and carried them out. They closely monitored the changes made and the outcomes were recorded and revisited. This developmental work allowed staff to reflect, plan, and monitor the children's welfare and learning. It became an integral part of the ongoing center development plans and policies in both centers.

After 2 years of such development, the center heads agreed to take part in an external validation exercise wherein another trained researcher came into the center, without any prior knowledge of it, and rated it for its environmental quality, using both the ECERS-R and ECERS-E. Both centers scored an average of 6 on both scales, placing them between good and excellent on both. They are continuing to use the scales and are also looking at ITERS (*Infant and Toddler Environmental Rating Scale*) to engage in self-assessment and the development of their practice with the children who are under 3 years old.

What has been learned from this experience? When interviewed as part of their annual evaluation, both head teachers made it clear that they had taken the exercise very seriously. When asked why she undertook this trial in her center, Bernadette Duffy, Head of Thomas Coram and Coram Parents' Early Excellence Center, replied:

> "It's about being brave enough to be objective, it's about being self-critical and hard on yourself."

Lynn Kennington, Head of Gamesley Early Excellence Center, said,

> "The discussion process is the best, we got quite high scores but we could be doing better than even what's measured, we as staff are not entirely happy with this and feel we could go further."

Clearly then the ECERS can be used effectively as a self-assessment and improvement tool at preschool centers or reception class levels (the 1st year of compulsory schooling) as long as the following criteria are met:

- rigorous training is provided on both the quality criteria (definitions and cultural variations) and on the use and the role of the scales
- it is recognized that an exercise of this nature requires a critical mass of reflective practitioners within the setting
- a critical friend supports the initiative (an insider, e.g., a local authority advisor or a representative from Higher Education. In the cases of Gamesley and Thomas Coram centers, their external evaluator also acted as critical friend).
- there is a willingness to undergo external validation in the form of "blind" assessment by a trained, reliable assessor.

We are grateful to the staff and the head teachers of Gamesley and Thomas Coram EECs for their time and efforts in using the ECERS instruments and in helping us to understand how they can best be used by centers as a self-assessment tool.

Improvement at the State/Federal Level

The ECERS-R and ECERS-E can support leaders and practitioners in implementing quality improvement by providing an empowering tool that offers a clear and concrete path for them to follow (see Mathers et al., 2007). This has been particularly important in U.K. settings, which are inspected under the Office for Standards in Education. Pending an inspection, leaders of early-years settings have to provide information on a Self Evaluation Form (SEF), and ECERS has been invaluable in helping such leaders to chart their "improvement journey." But the scales can also bring major benefits to state/federal early childhood initiatives and programs. In the United Kingdom, the ECERS-R and ECERS-E are used extensively to support

- quality improvement and self-assessment: a tool for advisers and consultants who work with centers and identify priorities for improvement;
- quality assurance: as a Quality Assurance framework in its own right, or alongside existing schemes;
- audits to provide information at the state/federal level by mapping

quality trends across the state/federation to prioritize spending, training, and support;

- measuring change: e.g., assessing the impact of new initiatives.

The following illustrates how both ECERS have been used effectively at a regional level. England is divided into 154 regions, referred to as "Local Authorities." While they all have to adhere to nationwide laws and regulations for early-years centers (e.g., a national curriculum, national safety regulations, etc.), they do have some local flexibility in how they manage and deliver these national standards. This differs considerably from the U.S. context, where there is more flexibility as individual states can set their own standards. NAEYC has an accredited program that is available nationwide, but this is voluntary. There are federal programs that aim to supply more money, either directly to states or in the form of tax incentives, for expanded and improved early childhood education and care. This may eventually lead to a more coherent set of standards across state boundaries.

How ECERS can be used at a state level can best be described by how it is currently used by Local Authorities in the U.K. context, as illustrated in two brief examples. One such authority is Derbyshire, located in the relatively economically deprived north of England. In 2007 Derbyshire had a population of 40,000 children under 5 (Office of National Statistics, www.statistics.gov.uk).

Derbyshire's local inspectors were working in partnership with centers to complete an audit, and they used ECERS-R and ECERS-E as quality improvement tools. Attracted by the international reputation of the scales, the Authority is in the first year of a phased roll-out of the scales to its 300 public schools and an additional 300 private, voluntary, and independent settings. "We saw the scales as the next step in encouraging reflective practice in our schools and settings, and as a way to build knowledge and confidence among practitioners. They are tools that give settings . . . a clear idea of what they are good at, what they need to change, and how to get there" (Sue Ricketts, Senior Adviser, Education Improvement, Derbyshire County Council).

Similarly, the Early Years and Childcare Service of Surrey Local Authority (in the more affluent south of England), with a population in 2007 of 52,200 children under 5 (Office of National Statistics, www.statistics.gov.uk), have used ECERS-R and ECERS-E audits to target support and measure improvements in settings as part of an Authority-wide audit of its 500 private, voluntary, and independent settings. As part of their self-evaluation process, leaders, in consultation with their staff, are expected to use the scales to set targets and put together action plans to improve the quality of provision.

The use of ECERS-R and ECERS-E, whether at the Authority or setting level, should be a transparent, inclusive, and positive experience that involves and empowers staff and harnesses their enthusiasm for excellent practice.

Inadequate		Minimal		Good		Excellent
1	2	3	4	5	6	7

LITERACY

1. Print in the Environment

1.1 No labeled pictures are visible to the children.* D

1.2 No environmental print that is relevant to children on display.* D

3.1 A few labeled pictures are present and visible to children.* D

3.2 A few labeled objects or items are present and easily visible to the children (Ex. labels on shelves, children's names on coat hooks or paintings, containers labeled "pens," "pencils").*

3.3 Printed words are prominently displayed (Ex. "welcome" on the door, titles on art displays, labels designating interest centers within the room, such as the art area or sand/water area.)* D

5.1 Many labeled pictures are on view to the children, indicating a print-rich environment.* D

5.2 Children are encouraged to recognize printed words in their environment (Ex. their own names on peg labels, print on everyday objects, such as food packaging or shopping bags).*

5.3 Children are encouraged to recognize letters in their environment (Ex. staff draw attention to the individual letters in a child's name, or in other environmental print).*

7.1 Discussion of environmental print takes place and often relates to objects of personal interest to the children.*

7.2 There is discussion of the relationship between the spoken and the printed word (Ex. discussing how to read the words written on a child's T-shirt).*

7.3 Children are encouraged to recognize letters and words in their environment other than their own names (Ex. in words on labels or posters).*

---

*Notes for Clarification

Item 1. Environmental print includes all printed words in the child's environment, including words that are attached or superimposed on an object that has meaning to the child. To be truly "environmental," it must have meaning relevant to the object it relates to, for example, storage signs that include a picture and the name of the stored items, labels on shelves/children's pegs, print on packaging/clothing/shopping bags, printed instructions on picture signs ("please wash your hands"). These can be hand-written as well as printed.

Words that form part of resources (Ex. books, games, flashcards) are not considered to be "environmental print," since they have no illustrative meaning attached to the words. Do not count displays or other text that are relevant to adults rather than to children.

"Labeled pictures" (1.1/3.1/5.1): Do not count print without pictures. Pictures must be accompanied by brief text relating to the content of the picture (Ex. a poster of a car with the word "car" printed below, drawer labels with pictures *and* text labels to identify the contents). The text must be in large enough print to be read from a distance, and to be read by the children.

3.1. Two or more different examples.

3.2. Two or more different examples.

3.3. Print may be above eye level but children should be able to see it easily.

5.1. To give credit, at least five or more different examples should be present and easily visible to the children. The observer should be satisfied that the environment is "print-rich" in order to give credit.

5.2. To give credit, staff should be observed explicitly encouraging children to recognize environmental print (at least one example observed) or the observer should see evidence of a regular daily routine that encourages children to recognize print in the environment (Ex. a self-check-in system, where children find their names and post them on a board to show that they are present).

5.3. At least one example of adults drawing explicit attention to letters should be observed.

7.1. Discussions must actively involve children and be more extensive than a "passing mention." At least two examples must be observed, one of which must relate to an item clearly of personal interest to the children (Ex. a child's T-shirt, print on postcards sent by other children in the group, print on an object a child has brought in from home).

7.2. Discussion must actively involve children. At least one example should be observed.

7.3. To give credit, observers should see at least one example of staff encouraging children to recognize words in the environment, and at least one example of staff encouraging children to recognize letters.

Inadequate		Minimal		Good		Excellent
1	2	3	4	5	6	7

2. Book and Literacy Areas

1.1 Books are unattractive.*

1.2 Books are not of a suitable age level.*

3.1 Some books of different kinds are accessible to children.*

3.2 An easily accessible area of the room is set aside for books.*

3.3 Some reading takes place in the book area.*

5.1 A variety of types of books are accessible to children.*

5.2 Book area used independently by children.*

7.1 Book area is comfortable (rug and cushions or comfortable seating) and filled with a wide range of books of varied style, content, and complexity.*

7.2 Adults encourage children to use books and direct them to the book area.*

7.3 Books are included in learning areas outside of the book corner.*

---

*Notes for Clarification

1.1. This refers to the books themselves and not the way in which they are displayed. Score yes if 50% or more of the books are damaged.

1.2. Score "Yes" if 50% or more of the books are of an unsuitable age level.

3.1. Possible categories include: picture/story books, reference/information books, poetry/nursery rhymes, and counting/math books. Not all categories are required, but at least three or four examples from two different categories should be accessible to children daily.

3.2. The book area may also be used for other quiet activities and/or for whole-group time at certain times of the day, but must generally be intended for the purposeful reading of books.

3.3. This could be during whole-group time or informally, by groups or individual children, with or without adults. This indicator is specifically concerned with how extensively the book area (or areas) are used. Do not give credit if books are taken from the book area and used elsewhere (Ex. children select books from the book corner to read at the table while waiting for snack).

5.1. See 3.1 for possible categories of books. Books can be commercially produced or home-made. At least three examples from each category should be accessible to children daily (and observers should also base their decision on the highest number of children attending at one time). In addition, the selection should include many books with text, and some variation in the level of books available to represent different abilities (Ex. some simpler and some more complex, dual language texts or books in other languages where the group is diverse).

5.2. At least two (different) examples must be observed. However, observers should also base their judgment on the size of the group when determining whether children regularly access the book area independently of adults. Children must be accessing the book area for the purpose of selecting and reading books rather than for any other activity.

7.1. In addition to the variety of types required for 5.1, this indicator requires variety *within* the types of book offered to accommodate a range of interests (Ex. information books about science topics, transportation topics, and different cultures/religions; story books about animals, people, and imaginary creatures). Sizes and formats should vary. A greater variation in developmental level is also required than is necessary at 5.1. The area should contain books at many different levels, ranging from simple board books and books with many pictures/little text, to more complex books with a lot of text on each page and other more complex features (Ex. reference books with diagrams).

7.2. This should be observed at least once.

7.3. Books should be provided in at least two other areas to give credit and should have some connection to the learning/play experiences provided in that area (Ex. counting books in the math area).

27

Inadequate		Minimal		Good		Excellent
1	2	3	4	5	6	7

3. Adult Reading with the Children

1.1 Adults rarely read to the children.* P, Q

3.1 Adults read with children daily.* P, Q

3.2 There is some involvement of the children during reading times (Ex. children are encouraged to join in with repetitive words and phrases in the text, adult shares pictures with the child/ren or asks simple questions).*

5.1 Children take an active role during reading times, and the words and/or story are usually discussed.*

5.2 Children are encouraged to think about and consider "what if" questions, and/or link the content of the book to other experiences.*

7.1 There is discussion about print and letters as well as content.*

7.2 There is support material for the children to engage with stories by themselves (Ex. tapes, interactive displays, puppets, story activity bags, computer games). D

7.3 There is evidence of one to one reading with some children. *

Notes for Clarification

1.1. Score "Yes" if no reading with the children is seen during the observation and there is no daily reading time listed on the schedule.

3.1. Give credit if two or more examples of informal reading with groups or individual children are seen during the observation. Alternatively, credit can be given if there is evidence of a planned daily reading time that includes all (or the majority of) the children, even if this happens outside the observation time. This could include whole-group reading or planned small-group reading times.

3.2. Reading with children must be observed on at least one occasion in order to score this indicator. If several reading times are observed, involvement of children should be a feature of the majority of sessions in order to give credit.

5.1. This must be observed at least once. If several reading sessions are observed, this should be true for most sessions.

5.2. Examples might include an adult asking: "What do you think [the character] will do next?" or (when reading a factual book about pets) "Do any of you have a pet at home? How do you take care of them?" If several reading sessions are observed, this should be true for most sessions.

7.1. This should be observed at least once to give credit.

7.3. Several examples should be observed. It should be clear that informal reading with individual children is a regular part of the daily routine.

Inadequate		Minimal		Good		Excellent
1	2	3	4	5	6	7

4. Sounds in Words*

1.1 Few or no rhymes or poems are spoken or sung.* P, Q

3.1 Rhymes are often spoken or sung by adults to children.* P, Q

3.2 Children are encouraged to speak and/or sing rhymes.*

5.1 The rhyming components of songs/rhymes are brought to the attention of children.*

5.2 The initial sounds in words are brought to the attention of children.*

7.1 Attention is paid to the syllables in words (Ex. through clapping games, jumping, etc.).* P

7.2 Some attention is given to linking sounds to letters. * (P)

*Notes for Clarification

Item 4. *Rhymes* could include nursery rhymes and other rhyming songs, poems, rhyming games played on the computer, card games that involve rhymes, rhyming books, or phonics activities that include rhyme. Give credit for rhymes spoken or sung with small groups of children as well as for whole-group activities. If songs are used as evidence, credit can only be given if these are rhyming songs. Adults must be actively involved. For example, do not give credit if you see children listening to taped songs/rhymes by themselves.

1.1. Score "Yes" if there is evidence that rhymes are spoken or sung fewer than 2 or 3 times per week (Ex. only one singing time scheduled per week and no evidence of informal singing during the session observed).

3.1. "Often" means daily. Give credit if there is evidence of a planned daily singing/rhyme session that includes all (or the majority of) the children, even if this occurs outside the observation period. Depending on the number of children attending, this may be carried out in a small group rather than as a whole-class activity. If there is no daily group session planned, then at least two examples of informal use of rhyme (Ex. singing, rhyming books) with small groups or individual children should be seen during the observation.

3.2. It is not necessary for adults to draw explicit attention to rhyme to give credit at this level. For example, give credit if it is observed that children usually join in during singing sessions, or when reading a rhyming book.

5.1. At least one example must be observed.

5.2. At least two examples must be observed. Adults must draw explicit attention to the initial sounds in words and say the words out loud. (Ex. drawing attention to the fact that "bat" and "ball" start with the same letter, by saying "can you hear—they both begin with 'b.' Can you think of anything else which starts with the same letter?").

7.1. Give credit if this is seen during the observation. If no examples are observed on the day, then at least two examples should be found in the sample of the curriculum plans that are reviewed.

7.2. To give credit, observers should either see *two* examples of adults linking sounds to letters, or see *one* example and find two examples in the sample of the curriculum plans that are reviewed. Examples might include phonics work that makes the link between letters and sounds explicit, or an adult helping a child to write down a particular spoken word

Inadequate		Minimal		Good		Excellent
1	2	3	4	5	6	7

5. Emergent Writing/Mark-Making*

1.1 There are no materials for children to engage in emergent writing.*

1.2 Children never observe staff writing down what they (the children) say.* D, R

3.1 Children have access to writing materials (Ex. pencils, markers, chalks).

3.2 Children have access to paper or other resources appropriate to a writing task (Ex. pads of paper, chalk boards, small wipeable boards for use with dry wipe markers).

3.3 Children sometimes observe staff writing down what they (the children) say.* D, R

5.1 A place in the setting is set aside for emergent writing (Ex. a writing center).*

5.2 Children often observe staff writing down what they (the children) say.*

5.3 Children are encouraged to try "writing" to communicate with others (Ex. home-made books, written menus in the "restaurant," labeling their own picture).

7.1 As well as pencils and paper, the writing center/area has a theme to encourage children to "write" (Ex. an office).

7.2 Adults draw children's attention to the purpose of writing, (Ex. addressing an envelope, making a shopping list, writing a story).* D, R, (P)

7.3 Children's emergent writing is displayed for others to see.* D

---

*Notes for Clarification

Item 5. "*Emergent*" or "*developing*" writing is young children's own attempts at translating oral language into a written form. In its earliest stages it may appear as lines and squiggles, but if asked the child can usually tell you what they have "written." As children become more proficient, evidence of letters or numbers begins to emerge from this seemingly random mark making. Children copying what an adult has written is not considered emergent writing.

1.1. Score "Yes" if children do not have access to writing materials for at least some portion of the day.

1.2, 3.3, 5.2. Observers should check displays and children's records/portfolios for evidence of staff writing down children's spoken words. Examples might include children's art work displayed with their words written as a caption underneath.
  —For indicators 1.2 and 3.3, evidence from records and displays can be used.
  —To give credit at 1.2, one example should be found in the materials reviewed.
  —To give credit at 3.3, two examples are required.
  However, since there is no way of knowing whether the writing was actually shared with the child, evidence from records/displays is not adequate.

  To give credit for indicator 5.2. observers should see at least one example of an adult writing the words the children have spoken for them.

5.1. This must be a designated area (or areas) with suitable materials and space to write—it is not enough for children to have access to writing materials that they then take to any available table. A wider variety of materials to encourage mark making should also be available at this level (Ex. a writing area with pens, pencils, crayons, pads, rulers, calendars, and diaries; a dramatic play store with shopping lists, price tags, catalogs, pencils, and pads of paper).

7.2. Examples might include writing connected to dramatic play (Ex. labeling packages in a post office) or children contributing to environmental print (Ex. writing labels for their drawers or for displays). If a purposeful writing activity is not seen on the day, observers should look for evidence that such activities have taken place (Ex. displayed materials). At least 3 examples of purposeful writing should be found in the display and records reviewed. Confirmatory evidence can be sought in the planning. However, since the observer will not know how well planning is (or has been) carried out, credit for this indicator should not be given solely on the basis of planning evidence.

7.3. Do not give credit for writing that is copied/traced from an adult's handwriting.

Inadequate		Minimal		Good		Excellent
1	2	3	4	5	6	7

6. Talking and Listening

1.1 Very little encouragement or opportunity for children to talk to adults.

1.2 Most verbal attention from adults is of a supervisory nature.*

3.1 Some conversation between adults and children occurs (Ex. adults talk to the children either individually or as a group about an ongoing activity, ask simple questions, respond to children's comments).

3.2 Children are allowed to talk among themselves with some limited adult intervention (Ex. adults ask yes/no questions or supply one-word answers).

5.1 Interesting experiences are planned by adults and drawn upon to encourage talk and the sharing of ideas.* (P)

5.2 Children are encouraged to answer questions in a more extended way (requiring more than one-word answers).*

5.3 Adults regularly create one-to-one opportunities to talk with children by initiating conversations with individuals.*

7.1 Adults provide scaffolding for children's conversations with them.*

7.2 Children are often encouraged to talk to each other in small groups, and adults encourage their peers to listen to them.* P

7.3 Adults regularly use open-ended questions to extend the children's language through talk (Ex. "what do you think would happen if . . . ?" "How did you make . . . ?")*

7.4 Children are encouraged to ask questions.*

*Notes for Clarification

1.2. Score "Yes" if the majority of adult's talk is related to managing routines, activities, or behaviors.

5.1. This indicator assesses the extent to which adults plan for talk. Experiences must have an explicit focus on communication and the sharing of ideas. "Non-literacy" activities (Ex. science experiments) can be counted if there is a planned and explicit focus on discussion. Examples of appropriate planning might include listing key words or questions for a particular activity, or "brainstorming" at the beginning of a topic to gather children's ideas. As with all items, planning evidence should be used with caution and at least one planned activity must be observed to assess how effectively adults draw on the experience to encourage children's talk. If this is not the case, credit should not be given.

5.2. Credit can be given here for questions that require longer answers than "yes" or "no," but that are not as challenging as those required for indicator 7.3. (Ex. an adult might ask a child "Which animals are you going to put in the barn?" or "What are you going to wear for the party tomorrow?"). No specific number of examples is required but observers should hear enough evidence to be sure that such questions are a regular occurrence.

5.3. Several examples should be observed, and conversations with individual children should take place in a variety of contexts (Ex. during routines, during adult-led activities, during child-initiated free play). Conversations at this level should also be more extensive than is required for indicator 3.1 and should involve a number of back-and-forth communications between adult and child.

7.1. Scaffolding provides a "framework" for children's talk. To give credit, adults should be observed accepting and extending children's verbal contributions in conversation (Ex. child says "Look, the beans are growing," and the adult responds "Yes, that's right, they're growing really tall. How tall do you think they will get?"). No specific number of examples is required, but observers should hear enough evidence to be sure that extending children's thinking through questioning or strategic commenting is a regular occurrence.

7.2. The emphasis here is on small groups—do not count whole-group discussions/circle times when scoring this indicator. The communication should be more focused than simply talking while taking part in a play activity. Examples might include children talking about a picture they have painted or recalling a trip outside the center. If planning is used as evidence, the observer should be satisfied that the talk is likely to be of good quality, and that children are encouraged to listen to one another (i.e., evidence from other observations should support this conclusion).

7.3. No specific number of examples is required but observers should hear enough evidence to be sure that such questions are a regular occurrence.

7.4. At least one explicit example of encouragement must be observed. In addition, where children do ask questions spontaneously, adults should respond in an encouraging and respectful way (Ex. give the child time to ask the question, respond with interest to the question).

MATHEMATICS

Note: Items 7 and 8 *must* be completed. After assessing Items 7 and 8 you may then select *either* Item 9a or Item 9b for evidence. You may choose the item that is most apparent during the observation. This mathematics subscale may require access to curriculum planning documents.

7. Counting and the Application of Counting*

1.1 Children rarely take part in activities or routines where counting is used.* P, D, R, Q

1.2 Very few resources are available to encourage the children to take part in counting activities (Ex. acorns, shells, buttons, counting books, games).*

3.1 A few number activities, counting books, games, songs, or rhymes are used with the children.* P, D, R, Q

3.2 Numbers are named as part of daily routines.*

3.3 Math materials include a few resources that encourage children to take part in counting activities (Ex. posters featuring numbers, sets of countable objects, counting books, games or other resources).* D

5.1 Number activities such as songs, rhymes, counting books and/ or games are often used with the children.* (P), (D), (R)

5.2 Children are encouraged to count objects and to associate the spoken numbers with the numerical concepts (Ex. counting the number of children present at arrival, counting out six milk cartons for six children, asking a child to count the number of blocks in a tower they have made).*

5.3 Adults use ordinal numbers (1st, 2nd, 3rd . . .) when working with the children.*

7.1 All children are actively encouraged to take part in counting objects in a variety of contexts (Ex. dramatic play, snack time, sharing Legos).*

7.2 Activities are planned that encourage one-to-one correspondence, both indoors and outdoors (or outside the setting).* P

7.3 Adults incorporate into their curriculum planning working with children on specific number activities (Ex. dice games, dominoes, matching numbers to numbers or numbers to pictures).* P

7.4 There is a well-equipped math area with number games, countable objects, and books.*

(Notes for Clarification on next page)

Item 7. "Number activities" could include: counting songs/rhymes; counting books; counting games; computer/interactive whiteboard programs that include counting; use of math resources such as a number line during whole-group sessions. Observers should also give credit for incidental counting during play. In theory, any play activity is acceptable if adults make counting an explicit and significant part of the activity (i.e. more than a "passing mention" of number). Activities should be culturally and developmentally appropriate. For example, rote counting or use of worksheets with no concrete experiences cannot be counted as evidence of number activities.

"Daily routines" are non-play-based and might include snack or lunchtime, arrival, putting coats on and lining up to go outside, clean-up time. Use of number during routine activities might include, for example, working out how many plates are needed for snack time, counting the number of children present at arrival, or counting the number of steps to the playground when going outdoors.

1.1. Score "Yes" if there is evidence that children have access to appropriate counting experiences in any form (i.e., during number activities or routines) less than once per week.

1.2. Score "Yes" if there are fewer than three resources (or sets of resources) available. Resources do not need to be accessible daily to give credit. Sets must contain enough objects to be useable as part of a counting activity.

3.1. "A few" means once a week or more (daily math activities are not required at this level). See definition above for examples of number activities.

3.2. At least one example must be observed.

3.3. At least two examples should be accessible on a daily basis to give credit.

5.1. "Often" means daily. Number activities must be seen during the observation to give credit for this indicator. Give credit if at least two examples of spontaneous counting activities with groups or individual children are observed (see *All About the ECERS-E* [Mathers & Linskey, forthcoming] for further detail). Alternatively, give credit if there is evidence of a daily math activity that includes all children, even if you notice adults missing other incidental opportunities for math learning during the observation. The observer does not need to see examples from all categories (i.e., songs, rhymes, counting books and games) during the observation in order to give credit. However, confirmatory evidence should be sought in the planning, records and display to ensure that all these options are offered at some time.

5.2. At least two examples should be observed. These could take place during group time or free play. Adults must be observed encouraging the children to count.

5.3. At least one example should be observed. Look for evidence of ordinal numbers being used during everyday activities (Ex. talking about who will be first/second/third during a turn-taking game; counting through what day of the week it is).

7.1. To give credit at this level, staff should be looking beyond the obvious situations that lend themselves to counting, and bringing the concept of number into a wide range of contexts (both formal and informal), with small groups and individuals as well as with the whole group. Several instances should be observed in different contexts.

7.2. To give credit, at least three different examples of activities that explicitly encourage one to one correspondence must be found in the sample of planning reviewed, at least one of which must relate to outdoor activities/play.

7.3. To give credit, specific number activities should be explicitly planned for several times per week.

7.4. Number games, countable objects, and books should be accessible to children on a daily basis.

Inadequate		Minimal		Good		Excellent
1	2	3	4	5	6	7

8. Reading and Representing Simple Numbers

1.1 Attention is not paid to the reading and/or representation of simple numbers.* P, D, R

1.2 No written numbers are displayed.* D

3.1 Numbers and the equivalent objects are shown next to each other (Ex. a number poster showing the number "1" next to one apple, the number "2" next to two pears, etc.). D

3.2 Some children occasionally read and/or represent numbers.* P, D, R

3.3 Children's attention is drawn to written number sequence (Ex. by a number line or by talking to the children about a counting book).*

5.1 Children are regularly encouraged to read and/or represent simple numbers.* (D), (P), (R)

5.2 Children have materials available that support them in representing numbers (Ex. number shapes).*

7.1 There are planned classroom activities containing numbers and adults encourage children to recognize and represent numbers in a variety of media.* (D), (P), (R)

7.2 Written number work is linked to a practical purpose (Ex. putting the age on a birthday card).* D, P, R

(Notes for Clarification on next page.)

Item 8. Children's use of written number at this age should be "emergent number," i.e., young children's own attempts at representing and recording numbers in a written form. In its earliest stages it may appear as lines and squiggles, or simple "tallying." For older children, this might involve writing a shopping list in the housekeeping area and listing how many of each item are needed. Formal writing of numbers is not suggested for children in the ECERS-E age range. Written number work should be linked to a practical purpose and to concrete experiences (Ex. pricing items in a dramatic play shop) rather than through formal activities and/or worksheets.

1.1. Score "Yes" if there is no evidence during the observation, or in planning/records/display, that adults draw children's attention to written numbers, or that opportunities for children to recognize and/or represent numbers are provided.

1.2. Numbers should be easily visible to children, i.e., at eye level, or large enough to read from a distance.

3.2. Evidence is not required for all children in the group. To give credit, observers should find at least one example of a child (or children) reading number and/or one example of a child (or children) representing number—either during the observation, or in the sample of materials (planning, records and display) reviewed.

3.3. At least one example must be observed. Adults should be observed drawing explicit attention to written numbers in sequence, and the numbers should also be spoken aloud so that children associate spoken numbers with the written concepts. This could take place at whole group time, or informally with small groups or individual children.

5.1. Opportunities must be available within the environment that allow and encourage children to recognize and represent numbers (where appropriate). Observers should look for supporting evidence in the environment, display, planning, or records that these opportunities are available regularly (if not daily, then at least three times per week). In addition, at least one example of adults explicitly encouraging recognition or representation of number must be observed. This may take place during whole-group time or during child-initiated play.

5.2. These do not need to be accessible daily.

7.1. Number activities must be planned at least weekly in order to give credit. In addition, observers should see at least two examples of children being encouraged to recognize or write/represent simple numbers in different contexts/media (Ex. drawing numbers in sand, with paint, reading or writing numbers on the computer, reading numbers in the environment.

7.2. This indicator requires that children are encouraged to use numbers for a practical purpose in order to support their activities within the setting. If this is not observed on the day, at least two examples must be found in the materials reviewed.

Inadequate		Minimal		Good		Excellent
1	2	3	4	5	6	7

Select either Item 9a or 9b for evidence: Choose the one that is most apparent during the observation.

9a. Mathematical Activities: Shape

1.1 Little evidence that children have opportunities to experience or learn about shape (Ex. shape is rarely commented on during ordinary play or daily routines, adults do not plan activities that involve shapes).* P, D, R

3.1 Some different shapes are accessible to children.*

3.2 Shapes are named outside planned shape activities.*

3.3 Shape is an explicit part of some activities.* P, D, R

5.1 A wide variety of shapes are accessible and adults draw children's attention to shape names (Ex. circle, square, triangle, rectangle).*

5.2 Staff draw children's attention to shape in their own work (Ex. drawings, models).*

7.1 Many activities and materials are available which encourage children to generalize shape across a variety of contexts (Ex. art activities, construction activities, group-play arrangements, dramatic play).* (P), (R), (D)

7.2 Activities develop and extend concepts beyond basic shapes (Ex. to include properties of two- or three-dimensional shapes). P, R, D

7.3 Staff encourage children to understand the properties of different shapes (Ex. 3 sides of a triangle) and to use this understanding to solve shape puzzles and apply their knowledge to new situations.* D, P, R

---

*Notes for Clarification

1.1. Score "Yes" if no references to shape are seen during the observation and there is no evidence in planning, records or display that shape work has been carried out in the past.

3.1. Any resources with different shaped pieces can be counted (Ex. blocks with different shaped pieces, shape cutters for cooking/play dough activities, shapes displayed on the wall). At least two examples should be accessible on a daily basis to give credit.

3.2. Staff members are not required to use the proper names for shapes, to give credit for this indicator, common names are acceptable (Ex. tube). Other pattern-related language is also acceptable as evidence (Ex. pointy, wavy). At least one example of staff using shape or pattern language should be observed to give credit.

3.3. Give credit if an explicit shape activity is observed. If planning, records or display are used as evidence, at least two different examples must be found in the sample of materials reviewed.

5.1. A good selection of shape resources (5 or more examples) should be accessible on a daily basis to give credit (Ex. a shape poster, a set of shape puzzles, a set of 3D shapes, a set of blocks of different shapes, a book on shapes in the book area). Others may be available but not accessible daily. A wider variety of different shapes should also be accessible than is expected in indicator 3.1. In addition to the availability of resources, observers should hear at least two examples of adults drawing attention to shape names.

5.2. At least one example must be observed.

7.1. At least three examples must be evident on the day of the observation, although confirmatory evidence can be found in the sample of materials reviewed.

7.3. The emphasis here is on applying knowledge of shape.

Inadequate		Minimal		Good		Excellent
1	2	3	4	5	6	7

9b. Mathematical Activities: Sorting, Matching, and Comparing

1.1 Children are not encouraged to sort, match, or compare objects and materials.* P, D, R

3.1 Some items to support sorting, comparing, and/or matching are accessible.*

3.2 Children sort, compare, and/or match by at least one identifiable criterion (Ex. heavy/light or by color).* P, D, R

3.3 Staff demonstrate sorting, comparing, or matching and allow the children to participate.*

5.1 Activities occur regularly that develop and extend sorting, comparing, and matching skills (Ex. sorting by more than one criterion, sorting in different contexts, using objects in the child's everyday environment).* (P)

5.2 Characteristics that form the basis for sorting, matching, and comparing are made explicit by the adults.

5.3 Staff encourage children to use comparative language when sorting, matching, comparing, or measuring (Ex. big, bigger, biggest, bigger/smaller).*

7.1 Children are encouraged to identify the characteristics of sets of objects that form the basis for sorting, matching, or comparing (Ex. explaining why a set of shapes is alike by saying, "They are all circles").*

7.2 Language that explores sorting, comparing, or matching is used in a variety of contexts across a range of activities (Ex. ordering the size of the three bears; using words such as curlier, bigger, heavier).*

7.3 Children are encouraged to complete a sorting/matching/comparing activity, then repeat it using a different criterion (including their own) as the basis for sorting/matching/comparing (Ex. arrange hats by size, then by shape).* P

---

*Notes for Clarification

1.1. Score "Yes" if no references to sorting, matching, or comparing are seen during the observation and there is no evidence in planning, records or display that such work has been carried out in the past.

3.1. Examples of items that could be matched, sorted, or compared include everyday objects such as collections of natural materials (Ex. pebbles, pine cones, shells) and different shaped or sized resources (Ex. containers for sand/water play, blocks) as well as the more commercial "counting" resources, such as counting bears, unifix cubes, or sorting/matching games. At least two examples should be accessible on a daily basis to give credit.

3.2. Give credit if children are observed sorting, matching, or comparing (with or without adults) during the observation. If planning, records, or display are used as evidence, at least two different examples must be found in the sample of materials reviewed.

3.3. At least one example should be observed, and must involve staff actively demonstrating or supporting sorting/matching/comparing. This might take place as part of a planned adult-led activity, or more informally with a small number of children (e.g., showing children how to sort resources when tidying away, pointing out the fact that two children have matching colored tops and encouraging them to identify others wearing the same color, encouraging a child to make a tower using only red blocks).

5.1. At least one example should be observed. Observers should also check planning for regularity ("regularly" means at least 3 to 4 times per week).

5.3. At least one example must be observed. The focus here is on staff encouraging children to use comparative language.

7.1. At least one example must be observed.

7.2. At least two different examples must be observed.

7.3. If this is not observed on the day, at least one explicit example must be seen in the sample of materials reviewed.

Inadequate		Minimal		Good		Excellent
1	2	3	4	5	6	7

SCIENCE AND ENVIRONMENT

Note: Items 10 and 11 *must* be completed. After completing Items 10 and 11, you may then select *either* Item 12a, Item 12b, or Item 12c for evidence. Choose the item that is most apparent during the observation. This science subscale may require access to planning documents.

10. Natural Materials*

1.1 There is little access indoors to natural materials (fewer than 3 examples).

3.1 Some natural materials are accessible to the children indoors.*

3.2 Natural materials are accessible outdoors.*

5.1 Natural materials are used beyond decoration to illustrate specific concepts (Ex. planting seeds or bulbs to illustrate growth, seed dispersal).* P, D

5.2 Children are often encouraged to explore the characteristics of natural materials.*

5.3 Adults show appreciation, curiosity, and/or respect for nature when with children (Ex. interest in fungi or worms, rather than fear or disgust).*

7.1 Children are encouraged to identify and explore a range of natural phenomena in their environment outside the center and talk about/describe them.* (P), (D)

7.2 Children are encouraged to bring natural materials into the center.* D, Q

7.3 Children are encouraged to make close observations of natural objects and/or to draw them.* P, D, R

---

*Notes for Clarification

Item 10. *Natural materials* include living things (Ex. plants, fish, hamsters, etc), collections of natural objects (Ex. pebbles, pine cones, shells, etc.) and other natural materials such as sand and water. Materials should be in their natural state and recognizable as coming from the natural environment.

3.1. At least five different examples should be accessible daily. Others may be available but not accessible daily (e.g., those which cannot be left out for safety reasons).

3.2. At least five different examples should be accessible daily. Examples might include: trees that are accessible to children; gardens/planting areas (Ex. herbs, vegetable plots); animals kept outdoors (Ex. rabbit, guinea pig).

5.1. Give credit if this is observed on the day of the observation. If evidence is taken solely from planning/display, at least two different examples should be evident in the materials reviewed. At this level, the planning should include an explicit reference to the idea/scientific concept being introduced (Ex. "observing and drawing butterflies over time to understand their life cycle" rather than "drawing butterflies").

5.2. "Often" means daily. Give credit if one or more examples are observed. This could include informal discussion (Ex. feeling the texture of a pebble found in the playground; looking at mini-beasts under stones) as well as planned activities (Ex. cutting up fruits to look at the seeds).

5.3. At least one example must be observed.

7.1. At least one discussion relating to natural phenomena/materials should be observed and children should be seen to take an active role in the discussion. Planning or display evidence can be used as supporting evidence that children are encouraged to explore a range of natural phenomena (Ex. weather, mini-beasts, plants, animals, trip to forest/woods). Planning should also provide some evidence of planning for talk (Ex. key vocabulary).

7.2. Give credit if an example is observed on the day of the observation (Ex. staff set up a nature trail in the garden and encourage children to find objects for discussion at group time). Credit can also be given for recent display evidence showing children bringing natural materials into the center (Ex. a pet from home; gathering leaves in autumn). If not observed or seen in display, an open-ended question can be asked, for example: "How do you collect the natural materials for your topics and/or displays?" or "Could you give me some examples of when children have brought in natural materials they were interested in?" Do not give credit unless specific examples can be provided.

7.3. Give credit if this is observed. If planning, records or display are used, at least one example should be evident in the sample of materials reviewed (and this should be explicit enough to suggest that children have been encouraged to observe natural materials closely).

Inadequate		Minimal		Good		Excellent
1	2	3	4	5	6	7

11. Areas Featuring Science/Science Materials

1.1 No evidence of science resources, displays, books, or activities.

3.1 Science provision includes a selection of items (Ex. magnets or hand lenses).*

3.2 Displays show evidence of natural change (Ex. seasons).* D

3.3 Display(s) that could be used to generate discussion about science in the world around us are visible to the children (Ex. posters of the body, life cycle of a butterfly).*

5.1 A variety of science equipment is accessible for children to use.*

5.2 There is evidence of collections of things with similar and/or different properties (Ex. things that roll, stretch, bounce, are made of plastic, of metal).*

5.3 Print resources go beyond story books to some reference books or material on science topics.*

7.1 A wide range of science equipment is available.*

7.2 A range of reference materials is available, including books, pictures, reference charts, and photographs.* D

7.3 A large and stimulating science area is set up for the children to use daily.

7.4 Science materials are featured in other areas, in addition to the one specifically set aside for science (Ex. outdoors).*

*Notes for Clarification

3.1. At least two examples should be accessible on a daily basis.

3.2. The intention of this indicator is that adults have made an effort to "bring the outdoors in" and/or provide an opportunity for children to consider changes in the natural world.

3.3. The display must have a science purpose (Ex. posters showing pets or a generic woodland scene would not be adequate).

5.1/5.2. By "equipment," we refer to specific material that has been bought for encouraging science (Ex. mirrors, lenses, prisms, magnifying glasses, containers for collecting insects, color paddles, a microscope, etc.).

5.1. "Variety" means more of each type of item (so that several children can use the materials at once) but also a greater variety of items than is required for 3.1. At least five different examples should be accessible daily to give credit. Only give credit for general sand and water materials (Ex. funnels/containers/plastic tubes) if there is evidence that these are used for the learning of science (Ex. exploring sinking and floating).

5.2. There must be evidence that collections have been put together on the basis of their scientific properties and not, for example, because they are all the same color. Collections do not need to be accessible daily.

5.3. At least five examples (Ex. five science books) should be accessible daily to give credit.

7.1. As required for 5.1, plus examples of more specialized science materials that relate to specific topics, e.g., color (colored lenses, color paddles), light (prisms, light boxes), or electricity (batteries, wires). These more specialized items do not need to be accessible to the children on a daily basis.

7.2. Examples of all four categories should be available within the setting and easily accessible to adults so that they can refer to them when needed. A smaller range (representing several of the categories) should be accessible to the children daily. Pictures might include posters or other display.

7.4. For example, a seaside dramatic play area supplemented with reference books on seaside creatures, a crab claw, and a hand lens so that the children can make close observations.

Inadequate		Minimal		Good		Excellent
1	2	3	4	5	6	7

Select one of Items 12a, 12b, or 12c for evidence: Choose the one for which you can find the most detailed evidence.

12a. Science Activities: Non-living*

1.1 Children are not encouraged to explore aspects of their physical environment and scientific words and concepts are not featured in discussions.* P, D, R

3.1 Some science exploration or experiments are carried out by adults or children (Ex. ice cubes put out in sun).* P, D, R

3.2 Scientific words and/or concepts are mentioned daily (Ex. discussing the weather; using the words "floating" and "sinking" at the water tray; talking about melting, pressure, why/how things move).*

5.1 Staff often plan and introduce appropriate scientific concepts (Ex. how materials change, magnetism, sinkers and floaters) and children handle materials.* P, D, R

5.2 Adults draw attention to characteristics or changes in materials (Ex. birthday candles melting).*

5.3 Children are encouraged to use more than one sense to explore non-living phenomena and talk about their experience (Ex. touch/smell as well as sight).*

7.1 Children have hands-on experience in varied science activities exploring non-living materials.* (P), (D), (R)

7.2 Children are encouraged to experience a range of scientific concepts/ideas.* P, D, R

7.3 Adults engage children in discussion about materials and their characteristics.*

7.4 Adults encourage children to ask questions.*

7.5 Adults support children in systematically seeking answers to questions.*

7.6 Children are encouraged to record results of scientific enquiry.

---

*Notes for Clarification

Item 12a. In order to assess the higher levels you must have observed staff interacting with children (e.g., at the sand/water table or other activity area). At these levels, evidence is being sought for engagement with children in scientific processes—i.e., close observation, raising questions/making guesses (hypothesizing), experimenting (see what happens), and communicating and interpreting results (why has this happened?).

1.1. Score "Yes" if no examples are observed and no evidence is found in the planning/records/display reviewed.

3.1. Give credit if this is observed. If planning, records or display are used as evidence, at least two different examples must be found in the sample of materials reviewed. Examples might include investigating the friction of different surfaces for toy cars or the insulation/absorbency properties of different materials (e.g., which material will keep our doll the warmest/driest?).

3.2. At least one example must be observed, and must relate to non-living processes. This could take place during a planned science activity, or during everyday/informal activities or play.

5.1. This indicator requires that staff plan for science learning. At least four different examples relating to non-living processes must be found in the sample of materials (planning, records, and display) reviewed. At this level, the planning should include an explicit reference to the idea/scientific concept being introduced (Ex. "investigating which materials are magnetic and non-magnetic"

rather than "magnet play"). The second part of the indicator requires that children have the opportunity to handle materials (i.e., that staff do not simply demonstrate experiments for children to watch).

5.2. Adults must be observed drawing attention either to characteristics or to change at least once to give credit (Ex. drawing attention to water evaporating from the ground on a hot day). At this level, the talk should be more scientific than is required for 3.2.

5.3. At least one example must be observed to give credit. As well as being encouraged to use more than once sense, children should also be encouraged to talk about their experience using descriptive language (Ex. "What does it smell like?").

7.1. In order to assess whether activities are introduced in a hands-on way, at least one science activity must have been observed (Ex. exploring magnets and magnetic objects)—although not all children need to have taken part on that day. Evidence from planning, records, and display should also be reviewed to assess the variety in "non-living" activities provided (and this evidence should also point to a hands-on approach for all children).

7.2. In order to give credit, a broader range of concepts and ideas should be evident in the materials reviewed than is required for indicator 5.1.

7.3, 7.4, 7.5. At least one example must be observed, but one or more high-quality interactions may provide examples of 7.3, 7.4, and 7.5.

Inadequate		Minimal		Good		Excellent
1	2	3	4	5	6	7

12b. Science Activities: Living Processes*

1.1 Children are not encouraged to explore aspects of their natural environment and scientific words and concepts are not featured in discussions. * P, D, R

3.1 Some science exploration or experiments are carried out by adults or children (Ex. growing seedlings, keeping tadpoles). * P, D, R

3.2 Scientific words and concepts are mentioned daily (Ex. plant growth, insect habitats, the cycle of life, caring for living things).*

3.3 There are living things present, either indoors or outdoors (Ex. plants, fish, snails).

5.1 Staff often plan and introduce appropriate scientific concepts and children handle materials.* P D R

5.2 Adults draw attention to characteristics or changes in the natural world (Ex. the life cycle of a butterfly, the ageing process, the different parts of a flower).*

5.3 Children are encouraged to use more than one sense to explore living phenomena and talk about their experience (Ex. touch/smell as well as sight)*

7.1 All children have hands-on experience with living things where appropriate.* (P), (D), (R)

7.2 Children are encouraged to experience a range of scientific concepts/ideas.* P, D, R

7.3 Adults engage the children in discussion about both plant and animal worlds and their characteristics.*

7.4 Adults encourage children to ask questions. *

7.5 Adults support children in systematically seeking answers to questions. *

7.6 Children are encouraged to record results of scientific enquiry.

Notes for Clarification

Item 12b. In order to assess the higher levels you must have observed staff interacting with children (e.g., in the outdoor area). At these levels, evidence is being sought for engagement with children in scientific processes—i.e., close observation, raising questions/making guesses (hypothesizing), experimenting (see what happens), and communicating and interpreting results (why has this happened?).

1.1. Score "Yes" if no examples are observed, and no evidence is found in the planning, records, and display reviewed.

3.1. Give credit if this is observed. If planning, records or display are used as evidence, at least two different examples relating to living processes must be found in the sample of materials reviewed.

3.2. At least one example must be observed, and must relate to living processes. This could take place during a planned science activity or during everyday/informal activities or play. Examples might include discussing pets owned by the children or looking at a spider found in the playground.

5.1. This indicator requires that staff plan for science learning. At least four different examples relating to living processes must be found in the sample of materials (planning, records and display) reviewed. At this level, the planning should include an explicit reference to the idea/scientific concept being introduced (Ex. "observing and drawing butterflies over time to understand their life cycle" rather than "drawing butterflies"). The second part of the indicator requires that children have the

opportunity to handle materials (i.e., that staff do not simply demonstrate experiments for children to watch).

5.2. To give credit, adults must be observed drawing attention either to characteristics or to change at least once. At this level, the talk should be more scientific than is required for 3.2.

5.3. At least one example must be observed to give credit. As well as being encouraged to use more than one sense, children should also be encouraged to talk about their experience using descriptive language (e.g., "What does it feel like?").

7.1. In order to assess whether activities are introduced in a hands-on way, at least one science activity must have been observed (Ex. planting seeds, hunting for and collecting mini-beasts)—although not all children need to be observed taking part. Evidence from planning, records and display should also be reviewed to assess the variety in "living-processes" activities provided (and this evidence should also point to a hands-on approach for all children).

7.2. In order to give credit, a broader range of concepts and ideas should be evident in the materials reviewed than is required for indicator 5.1.

7.3. At least one example of discussion relating to the plant world, and one to the animal world, must be observed to give credit.

7.3, 7.4, 7.5. At least one example must be observed but one or more high-quality interactions may provide examples of 7.3, 7.4, and 7.5.

Inadequate		Minimal		Good		Excellent
1	2	3	4	5	6	7

12c. Science Activities: Food Preparation*

1.1 No preparation of food or drink is undertaken with the children.* P D R Q

3.1 Food preparation is sometimes undertaken with the children.* P, D, R, Q

3.2 Some children have the opportunity to participate in food preparation.* P, D, Q

3.3 Some food-related discussion takes place when appropriate (Ex. staff and children talk about food at snack time or during a cooking activity).*

5.1 Food preparation/cooking activities are often provided.* P, D, R, Q

5.2 Most of the children have the opportunity to participate in food preparation.* P, D, R, Q

5.3 The staff lead discussion about the food involved and use appropriate language (Ex. melt, dissolve).*

5.4 Children are encouraged to use more than one sense (Ex. feel, smell, taste) to explore individual ingredients and talk about their experiences.*

7.1 A variety of cooking activities (in which all children have the opportunity to take part) is often provided.* P

7.2 The end result is attractive, edible, and valued (Ex. eaten by children, taken home).

7.3 The staff lead and encourage discussion on the process of food preparation and/ or question children about it (Ex. What did it look like before? What does it look like now? What has happened to it?).*

(Notes for Clarification on next page.)

Item 12c. In order to assess the higher levels, you must have observed staff interacting with children—e.g., at snack time or during a cooking activity. At these levels, evidence is being sought for engagement with children in scientific processes—i.e., close observation, raising questions/making guesses (hypothesizing), experimenting (see what happens), and communicating and interpreting results (why has this happened?).

"Food preparation" includes cooking activities and also the preparation of food for snack or meal times (for which children may observe or participate).

1.1. Score "Yes" if children do not have the opportunity to observe (or participate) in food preparation/cooking during the observation, there is no evidence in the planning, records and display reviewed that children are ever offered this experience, and (when asked) staff are not able to provide examples of such activities taking place.

3.1. This might include children observing a member of staff preparing food. If planning, records or display are used as evidence, at least two examples must be found in the sample of materials reviewed.

3.2. This may be spontaneous (Ex. some children helping to prepare food for snack or lunch time) or planned in advance (Ex. planned cooking activities). If planning, records or display are used as evidence, at least two examples must be found in the sample of materials reviewed.

3.3. At least one example must be observed. Examples at snack or meal time might include a discussion about burnt toast, new crackers, or food brought in by the children.

5.1/7.1. "Often" means approximately every 1 to 2 weeks (or more frequently). Credit can be given if food preparation activities are offered every 1 to 2 weeks (even if not all children have a chance to participate this frequently).

5.2. The majority of children should have an opportunity to take part in food preparation at least once every 1 to 2 weeks.

5.3. This must be observed at least once. At this level, the talk should be more scientific than is required for 3.3.

5.4. At least one example must be observed. As well as being encouraged to use more than one sense, children should also be encouraged to talk about their experience using descriptive language (e.g., "What does it smell like?").

7.3. This must be observed at least once. Children must be actively involved in the discussion, and staff should be observed supporting and scaffolding the children's scientific language and learning.

Inadequate		Minimal		Good		Excellent
1	2	3	4	5	6	7

DIVERSITY

13. Planning for Individual Learning Needs

Ask to see the records kept on individual children.

1.1 Activities and resources are not matched to different ages, developmental stages, or interests.* P, Q

1.2 Planning is not written down.* P

1.3 Written planning takes no account of specific individuals or groups. P

1.4 No records kept, or if records are kept, they describe activities rather than the child's response or success in that activity (Ex. completed checklists or samples of children's work). R

3.1 Some adaptation is made to address specific needs of individuals or groups (Ex. additional learning or English language support).* P, Q

3.2 Some of the written planning shows differentiation for particular individuals or groups.* P

3.3 Written records indicate some awareness of how individuals have responded to activities, or of the appropriateness of activities, (Ex. needs bilingual support, able to count to 2).* R

3.4 Staff shows some awareness of children as individuals (Ex. recognizing work of children of all abilities by encouragement or praise).

5.1 The range of activities provided draws on children's interests and includes all developmental stages and backgrounds, enabling all children in the group to participate to promote their success and learning.* P, Q

5.2 Daily plans are written with the specific aim of developing activities that will satisfy the interests and needs of each child, either individually or as groups.* P

5.3 Children are observed frequently and individual records are kept on their progress in areas of development.* R

5.4 Staff consistently draw children's attention to diversity in a positive way.* (D)

7.1 The planning and organization for social interaction enables children of all developmental stages and backgrounds to participate at an appropriate level in both individual and common tasks (Ex. pairing children of different ages and abilities for certain tasks).* Q, P

7.2 Planning sheets identify the role of the adult when working with individuals/ pairs/groups of children. Planning also shows a range of ability levels at which a task or activity may be experienced.* P

7.3 Observations and records of progress are used to inform planning.* P, R, Q

7.4 Staff specifically plan activities that draw the attention of the whole group to difference and abilities in a positive way (Ex. showing children who are disabled in a positive light, celebrating bilingualism).* P, D, R

(Notes for Clarification on next page)

Activities and planning

1.1/3.1/5.1/1.2/3.2/5.2. There should be evidence that differentiated activities and/or resources are offered to children with particular needs (e.g., those who do not speak English as their first language) and according to age and developmental stage.

— 1.1/3.1/5.1 relate to the provision/adaptation of activities and resources offered to children (whether these are planned or informal) and the extent to which these cater to differing needs.

— 1.2/3.2/5.2 specifically assess the extent to which differentiation is *planned for*.

Examples of appropriate differentiation can be found in *All About the ECERS-E* (Mathers & Linskey, forthcoming).

5.1/5.2. The range of activities should provide for all children (e.g. children of different ages/stages, children with English as a second language) and not simply those with identified special needs.

7.1. It may be necessary to ask about this as it will not always be apparent why children have been encouraged to work together on a task. For example: "Why have you encouraged those children to work together?" "Do you ever encourage particular children to work together? Why? Can you give some examples?"

7.2 The adult guidance should be more detailed than simply listing which adult works with which activity/group. Both elements of the indicator (i.e., the adult guidance and the range of capability levels) must be met in order to give credit.

Observations and record-keeping

3.3. At this level credit can be given for records/observations that show fairly minimal awareness of how individuals have coped with activities (or of the appropriateness of activities).

5.3. To give credit, children should be observed weekly (or almost weekly) in some form. This may take the form of post-it notes recording specific incidents or achievements, rather than formal observations. Records of progress do not need to be updated weekly.

7.3. It may be necessary to ask a question to establish whether this happens (for example, ask staff to provide or show specific examples of observations being used to inform planning).

Celebrating difference

3.4. Give credit if it is clearly part of usual practice to praise all children in the group regularly.

5.4. This indicator relates to celebration of differences among children in the group. To give credit, the discussion must be more specific than is required for 3.4 (e.g., drawing specific attention to a new skill a child has mastered; a sensitive discussion with the group at lunchtime about why a particular child doesn't eat meat; explaining in an appropriate way why a child with a disability needs to sit on a special chair). At least one example must be observed, and supporting evidence may also be found in display (e.g., children's work displayed with specific comments about their achievements).

7.4. This indicator goes beyond the children in the group to consider the celebration of difference more generally. Observers should check planning for evidence that celebration of difference and capability are specifically planned for (e.g., discussing blindness and deafness as part of a topic on senses). Evidence may also be found in display or in children's records. To give credit, at least one example of explicit planning for celebration of difference should be found in the materials reviewed.

Inadequate		Minimal		Good		Excellent
1	2	3	4	5	6	7

14. Gender Equality and Awareness

1.1 Where books, pictures, small play figures (Ex. Lego people, dolls and/or displays) portray gender, few of them challenge gender stereotypes.* D

1.2 The staff ignores or encourages stereotypical gender behaviors (Ex. only girls are praised for looking pretty or boys for being strong).*

3.1 Some books, pictures, small world figures, dolls, and/or displays that challenge gender stereotypes are accessible to the children (Ex. father looking after baby, female soldier, photos of both boys and girls playing with the large blocks).* D

3.2 Children's activities and behavior sometimes cross gender stereotypes (Ex. boys cooking or caring for dolls in the housekeeping area, girls playing outside on large riding toys).

5.1 Many books, pictures, small world figures, dolls, and/or displays show males and females in non-stereotypical roles (Ex. male childcare worker, woman changing a tire).* D

5.2 Participation in activities that cross gender boundaries is common practice and/or adults explicitly encourage this when necessary (Ex. all children are expected, but not forced, to join in construction and dance). * (Q)

5.3 Dress-up clothes encourage non-stereotypical roles (Ex. unisex nurse or police outfits; non-gendered clothing such as blue jeans).* (P), (Q)

7.1 The children's attention is specifically drawn to books, pictures, small world figures, dolls, and/or displays that show males and females in non-stereotypical roles, and/or specific activities are developed to help the children discuss gender.* P, Q

7.2 Staff are confident in discussing and challenging the stereotypical behaviors and assumptions of children.* Q

7.3 Male educators are employed to work with children and/or males are sometimes invited to work in the center with the children.* Q

(Notes for Clarification on next page.)

*Notes for Clarification

1.1. Only score "Yes" if there is very little (or no) evidence of resources that counter stereotypes, e.g. less than 1 in 10 (10%) of resources that portray gender. Credit can be given for resources of one type if these are plentiful enough (Ex. many books but no pictures, small world figures, dolls, or displays).

1.2. Only score "Yes" if several examples (or one very explicit example) of stereotyping, or of staff ignoring stereotypical behavior/comments are seen during the observation.

3.1. Overall, 10% (or more) of the resources that portray gender should be non-stereotypical to give credit. Examples from two of the five categories should be evident and accessible to children on a daily basis.

5.1. Overall, 20% (or more) of the accessible resources that portray gender should be non-stereotypical to give credit. Examples from three of the five categories should be evident and accessible on a daily basis (although many examples in every category are not required).

5.2. Observers should look for evidence that all children access activities and areas that might be associated with one gender (Ex. woodworking bench, playing with dolls in the housekeeping area, active gross motor play). If this is seen to be common practice, credit can be given. If, however, one gender appears to dominate a particular activity to the exclusion of others and staff do not act to address this (e.g., by encouraging boys to join play in the housekeeping area) then score down. It may be necessary to ask a question to discover any particular strategies employed (e.g., if certain times are set aside for girls to play on very active gross motor equipment). However, unless a very specific answer is given to any question asked, this indicator should be scored based on observed behavior of children and staff.

5.3. If appropriate dress-up clothes are seen to be available, but are stored so that they are not accessible to children daily, the observer should check planning or ask a question to discover how often they are made accessible. Give credit if dress-up clothes that encourage non-gender roles are accessible to children twice a week or more.

7.1. Give credit if one or more examples are observed. Observable examples might include staff reading and discussing stories like *The Paperbag Princess* or *Mrs. Plug the Plumber*, which challenge traditional role-models. If non-stereotypical books and resources are present but adults are not observed using them, ask a non-leading question such as "Did you choose these resources for a particular reason?" or "Could you give me an example of how you use these books/resources?" Credit can also be given if explicit evidence is found in the planning of activities to help children discuss gender (at least one example in the sample of planning reviewed).

7.2. If this is not observed, the indicator may be scored using a question (e.g., "What would you do if a child suggested girls were not allowed to play with the tools because 'fixing things is a man's job?'"). Alternatively, the observer might ask for examples of occasions when children have said something "sexist" and how this was dealt with. Unless a very specific answer is given to any question asked, this indicator should be scored based on what is observed.

7.3. If male educators are not employed to work with the children, credit can be given if men are invited in to the center to take part in activities with the children at least 3 times per year.

		Inadequate		Minimal		Good		Excellent
		1	2	3	4	5	6	7

15. Race Equality and Awareness

1.1 Books, pictures, small play figures (Ex. Lego people), dolls, and displays show little evidence of ethnic diversity in our society or the wider world.* D

1.2 Negative, stereotypical, or offensive images are on view to the children (Ex. stereotypical images of an African or African American; Native Americans shown with tomahawks looking threatening). D

3.1 The children sometimes play with toys, resources, or materials from cultures other than the ethnic majority.* P, D, R

3.2 Books, pictures, small world figures, dolls, and/or displays show people from a variety of ethnic groups.* D

5.1 Children play with toys, resources, or materials drawn from a range of cultures (Ex. range of appropriate and non-stereotypical dress-up clothes, cooking and eating utensils used in dramatic play, musical instruments).* (P)

5.2 Some books, pictures, small world figures, dolls, and/or displays show people from different ethnic groups in non-stereotypical roles (Ex. as scientists, doctors, engineers, office workers in suits).* D

5.3 Some images or activities show children that they have much in common with people from other cultural groups (Ex. images that stress physical similarities or similarities in rituals and day-to-day activities).* P, D

5.4 Staff intervene appropriately when a child or an adult in the setting shows prejudice.* Q

7.1 Staff develop activities for the purpose of promoting cultural understanding (Ex. attention is drawn to similarities and differences in things and people; different cultures are routinely brought into the projects or unit themes; visitors and performers reflect a range of cultures).* P, D, R, Q

7.2 Specific activities are developed to promote understanding of difference (Ex. paints are mixed to match skin tones to visibly show subtlety in differences).* P, D, R, Q

7.3 Educators who are culturally or linguistically diverse are employed in the center or are invited into the setting to work with children. Q

(Notes for Clarification on next page.)

*Notes for Clarification

1.1/3.1/5.1. Resources should be clearly visible and in areas frequently used by the children.

3.1. At this level the resources may not be out every day, but there should be evidence that stored/borrowed toys or resources (Ex. cooking utensils/foods, dress-up clothes, real or imitation musical instruments) from other cultures are sometimes used, for example boxes of resources available for celebration of different festivals during the year, or resources representing different cultures are accessible to children in the housekeeping area. Resources representing at least two cultures other than the majority culture should be available at some time (but not necessarily daily). If no toys or resources are accessible on the day of the visit, observers should look at stored resources, and also for evidence in planning, display and/or records, that such materials are available and used.

3.2. A variety of different ethnic, cultural, and/or religious groups should be represented (e.g., at least three) and examples should be found in two of the five categories listed (i.e., books, pictures, small world figures, dolls, and displays). If the group is diverse, photographs of the children themselves can be counted. At this level, credit can also be given for images that show tokenism or are stereotypical—e.g., other nationalities portrayed only in national dress; Africans shown only in a traditional rural setting; black dolls with white features; books such as Handa's Surprise in the book selection, but no stories or pictures of African children living in a western culture. Do not give credit for images that are offensive.

5.1. To give credit for this indicator, there should be evidence of more than occasional celebration of other cultures/festivals (which could appear to show tokenism and which can be credited in indicator 3.1). Race equality and multicultural awareness should be embedded in the ethos of the setting. Resources from two or more cultures should be accessible daily, and resources from at least two other cultures should be available at some time (but not necessarily daily). Planning can provide supporting evidence of the range of cultures included in day-to-day activities and celebrations.

5.2. At least three different examples should be visible/accessible daily (across at least 2 of the 5 categories).

5.3. Similarities and differences must be explicitly shown in display and/or planning. Children should receive a constant message that all children do similar everyday things (Ex. go to the park, attend weddings). Two or more examples are required in the display or planning reviewed.

5.4. If no prejudice is shown, use a question such as "What would you do if one of the children showed prejudice towards another, or made a racist remark?" Give credit for this indicator if the answer indicates a sensitive approach: The child should not be blamed, but told that their words and/or behavior are inappropriate/inaccurate. The adult should then provide a correct explanation and suggest a more appropriate response.

7.1/7.2. These indicators assess the extent to which staff use activities as a vehicle to take children beyond simple recognition and into understanding and respect of different races and cultures. For each indicator at least three explicit examples must be found in the materials reviewed (or provided as answers to questions).

ECERS-E SCORE SHEET

Center/School: _____ Date: _____ Observer: _____

Time observation began: _____ Time observation ended: _____

LITERACY	

1. Print in the environment `1 2 3 4 5 6 7`

	Y	N			Y	N			Y	N			Y	N	
1.1	☐	☐	D	3.1	☐	☐	D	5.1	☐	☐	D	7.1	☐	☐	
1.2	☐	☐	D	3.2	☐	☐		5.2	☐	☐		7.2	☐	☐	
				3.3	☐	☐	D	5.3	☐	☐		7.3	☐	☐	

4. Sounds in words `1 2 3 4 5 6 7`

	Y	N			Y	N			Y	N			Y	N	
1.1	☐	☐	P Q	3.1	☐	☐	P Q	5.1	☐	☐		7.1	☐	☐	P
				3.2	☐	☐		5.2	☐	☐		7.2	☐	☐	(P)

2. Book and literacy areas `1 2 3 4 5 6 7`

	Y	N			Y	N			Y	N			Y	N
1.1	☐	☐	3.1	☐	☐	5.1	☐	☐	7.1	☐	☐		
1.2	☐	☐	3.2	☐	☐	5.2	☐	☐	7.2	☐	☐		
			3.3	☐	☐				7.3	☐	☐		

5. Emergent writing/mark making `1 2 3 4 5 6 7`

	Y	N			Y	N			Y	N			Y	N	
1.1	☐	☐		3.1	☐	☐		5.1	☐	☐		7.1	☐	☐	
1.2	☐	☐	D R	3.2	☐	☐		5.2	☐	☐		7.2	☐	☐	D R (P)
				3.3	☐	☐	D R	5.3	☐	☐		7.3	☐	☐	D

3. Adult reading with the children `1 2 3 4 5 6 7`

	Y	N			Y	N			Y	N			Y	N	
1.1	☐	☐	P Q	3.1	☐	☐	P Q	5.1	☐	☐		7.1	☐	☐	
				3.2	☐	☐		5.2	☐	☐		7.2	☐	☐	D
												7.3	☐	☐	

6. Talking and listening `1 2 3 4 5 6 7`

	Y	N			Y	N			Y	N			Y	N	
1.1	☐	☐		3.1	☐	☐		5.1	☐	☐	(P)	7.1	☐	☐	
1.2	☐	☐		3.2	☐	☐		5.2	☐	☐		7.2	☐	☐	P
								5.3	☐	☐		7.3	☐	☐	
												7.4	☐	☐	

MATHEMATICS

7. Counting and the application of counting

1	2	3	4	5	6	7

	Y	N			Y	N			Y	N			Y	N	
1.1	❑	❑	P D R Q	3.1	❑	❑	P D R Q	5.1	❑	❑	(P D R)	7.1	❑	❑	
1.2	❑	❑		3.2	❑	❑		5.2	❑	❑		7.2	❑	❑	P
				3.3	❑	❑	D	5.3	❑	❑		7.3	❑	❑	P
												7.4	❑	❑	

9a. Shape

1	2	3	4	5	6	7	NA

	Y	N			Y	N		Y	N			Y	N	
1.1	❑	❑	P D R	3.1	❑	❑	5.1	❑	❑		7.1	❑	❑	(P R D)
				3.2	❑	❑	5.2	❑	❑		7.2	❑	❑	P R D
				3.3	❑	❑	P D R				7.3	❑	❑	D P R

8. Reading and representing simple numbers

1	2	3	4	5	6	7

	Y	N			Y	N			Y	N			Y	N	
1.1	❑	❑	P D R	3.1	❑	❑	D	5.1	❑	❑	(D P R)	7.1	❑	❑	(D P R)
1.2	❑	❑	D	3.2	❑	❑	P D R	5.2	❑	❑		7.2	❑	❑	D P R
				3.3	❑	❑									

9b. Sorting, matching, and comparing

1	2	3	4	5	6	7	NA

	Y	N			Y	N			Y	N			Y	N	
1.1	❑	❑	P D R	3.1	❑	❑		5.1	❑	❑	(P)	7.1	❑	❑	
				3.2	❑	❑	P D R	5.2	❑	❑		7.2	❑	❑	
				3.3	❑	❑		5.3	❑	❑		7.3	❑	❑	P

SCIENCE AND ENVIRONMENT

10. Natural materials
1 2 3 4 5 6 7

```
      Y  N              Y  N              Y  N              Y  N
1.1   ☐  ☐       3.1   ☐  ☐       5.1   ☐  ☐  P D    7.1   ☐  ☐  (P D)
                 3.2   ☐  ☐       5.2   ☐  ☐          7.2   ☐  ☐  D Q
                                 5.3   ☐  ☐          7.3   ☐  ☐  P D R
```

11. Areas featuring science/science materials
1 2 3 4 5 6 7

```
      Y  N              Y  N              Y  N              Y  N
1.1   ☐  ☐       3.1   ☐  ☐       5.1   ☐  ☐       7.1   ☐  ☐
                 3.2   ☐  ☐  D    5.2   ☐  ☐       7.2   ☐  ☐  D
                 3.3   ☐  ☐       5.3   ☐  ☐       7.3   ☐  ☐
                                                  7.4   ☐  ☐
```

12a. Science activities: Non-living
1 2 3 4 5 6 7 NA

```
      Y  N                  Y  N                  Y  N                  Y  N
1.1   ☐  ☐  P D R    3.1   ☐  ☐  P D R    5.1   ☐  ☐  P D R    7.1   ☐  ☐  (P D R)
                     3.2   ☐  ☐            5.2   ☐  ☐            7.2   ☐  ☐  P D R
                                          5.3   ☐  ☐            7.3   ☐  ☐
                                                                7.4   ☐  ☐
                                                                7.5   ☐  ☐
                                                                7.6   ☐  ☐
```

12b. Science activities: Living processes
1 2 3 4 5 6 7 NA

```
      Y  N                  Y  N                  Y  N                  Y  N
1.1   ☐  ☐  P D R    3.1   ☐  ☐  P D R    5.1   ☐  ☐  P D R    7.1   ☐  ☐  (P D R)
                     3.2   ☐  ☐            5.2   ☐  ☐            7.2   ☐  ☐  P D R
                     3.3   ☐  ☐            5.3   ☐  ☐            7.3   ☐  ☐
                                                                7.4   ☐  ☐
                                                                7.5   ☐  ☐
                                                                7.6   ☐  ☐
```

12c. Science activities: Food preparation
1 2 3 4 5 6 7 NA

```
      Y  N                    Y  N                    Y  N                    Y  N
1.1   ☐  ☐  P D R Q    3.1   ☐  ☐  P D R Q    5.1   ☐  ☐  P D R Q    7.1   ☐  ☐  P
1.2   ☐  ☐             3.2   ☐  ☐  P D Q      5.2   ☐  ☐  P D R Q    7.2   ☐  ☐
                       3.3   ☐  ☐             5.3   ☐  ☐             7.3   ☐  ☐
                                              5.4   ☐  ☐
```

DIVERSITY

13. Planning for individual learning needs | 1   2   3   4   5   6   7 |

	Y	N			Y	N			Y	N			Y	N	
1.1	☐	☐	P Q	3.1	☐	☐	P Q	5.1	☐	☐	P Q	7.1	☐	☐	Q P
1.2	☐	☐	P	3.2	☐	☐	P	5.2	☐	☐	P	7.2	☐	☐	P
1.3	☐	☐	P	3.3	☐	☐	R	5.3	☐	☐	R	7.3	☐	☐	P R Q
1.4	☐	☐	R	3.4	☐	☐		5.4	☐	☐	(D)	7.4	☐	☐	P D R

14. Gender equality and awareness | 1   2   3   4   5   6   7 |

	Y	N			Y	N			Y	N			Y	N	
1.1	☐	☐	D	3.1	☐	☐	D	5.1	☐	☐	D	7.1	☐	☐	P Q
1.2	☐	☐		3.2	☐	☐		5.2	☐	☐	(Q)	7.2	☐	☐	Q
								5.3	☐	☐	(P Q)	7.3	☐	☐	Q

15. Race equality and awareness | 1   2   3   4   5   6   7 |

	Y	N			Y	N			Y	N			Y	N	
1.1	☐	☐	D	3.1	☐	☐	P D R	5.1	☐	☐	(P)	7.1	☐	☐	P D R Q
1.2	☐	☐	D	3.2	☐	☐	D	5.2	☐	☐	D	7.2	☐	☐	P D R Q
								5.3	☐	☐	P D	7.3	☐	☐	Q
								5.4	☐	☐	Q				

ECERS-E Profile

Center/School: _____   Observation 1: __ __ / __ __ / __ __   Observer(s): _____
                                                              m m   d d   y y

Teacher(s)/Classroom: _____   Observation 2: __ __ / __ __ / __ __   Observer(s): _____
                                                                m m   d d   y y

1 2 3 4 5 6 7

I. Literacy
(1–6)

Obs. 1   Obs.2
[   ]   [   ]
Average subscale score

1. Print in the environment
2. Book and literacy areas
3. Adult reading with the children
4. Sounds in words
5. Emergent writing/mark making
6. Talking and listening

II. Mathematics
(7–9b)

[   ]   [   ]

7. Counting and the application of counting
8. Reading and representing simple numbers
9a. Mathematical activities: Shape
9b. Mathematical activities: Sorting, matching, and comparing

III. Science and environment
(10–12c)

[   ]   [   ]

10. Natural materials
11. Areas featuring science/science materials
12a. Science activities: Non-living
12b. Science activities: Living processes
12c. Science activities: Food preparation

IV. Diversity
(13–15)

[   ]   [   ]

13. Planning for individual learning needs
14. Gender equality and awareness
15. Race equality and awareness

Average subscale scores

LITERACY
MATHEMATICS
SCIENCE AND ENVIRONMENT
DIVERSITY

1 2 3 4 5 6 7

Appendix A: Overview of the Subscales and Items of the ECERS-R

Space and Furnishings

1. Indoor space
2. Furniture and routine care, play, and learning
3. Furnishing for relaxation and comfort
4. Room arrangement for play
5. Space for privacy
6. Child-related display
7. Space for gross motor play
8. Gross motor equipment

Personal Care Routines

9. Greeting/departing
10. Meals/snacks
11. Nap/rest
12. Toileting/diapering
13. Health practices
14. Safety practices

Language-Reasoning

15. Books and pictures
16. Encouraging children to communicate
17. Using language to develop reasoning skills
18. Informal use of language

Activities

19. Fine motor
20. Art
21. Music/movement
22. Blocks

Activities *(continued)*

23. Sand/water
24. Dramatic play
25. Nature/science
26. Math/number
27. Use of TV, video, and/or computers
28. Promoting acceptance of diversity

Interaction

29. Supervision of gross motor activities
30. General supervision of children (other than gross motor)
31. Discipline
32. Staff-child interactions
33. Interactions among children

Program Structure

34. Schedule
35. Free play
36. Group time
37. Provision for children with disabilities

Parents and Staff

38. Provisions for parents
39. Provisions for personal needs of staff
40. Provisions for professional needs of staff
41. Staff interaction and cooperation
42. Supervision and evaluation of staff
43. Opportunities for professional growth

Appendix B: Reliability and Validity in the ECERS-E

The ECERS-E was developed specifically for assessing curricular aspects of quality, including pedagogy, in preschool centers subject to the national Early Childhood Curriculum for England. Multi-level statistical analyses revealed that the quality of center-based environment as measured by the ECERS-E, was a significant predictor of children's development at entry to school after controlling for pretest, child characteristics, and family background (Sylva et al., 2006). As demonstrated in the EPPE (http://eppe.ioe.ac.uk) and the Millennium Cohort (http://www.cls.ioe.ac.uk/studies.asp?section= 000100020001) studies (Mathers, Sylva, & Joshi, 2007), the ECERS-E is a reliable and valid instrument for assessing the educational aspects of program quality and is a significant predictor of children's cognitive, linguistic, and social-behavioral development.

The ECERS-E curricular extension scales were developed for the EPPE research project specifically to address the educational/curricular aspects of "quality," that are assessed in less detail in the ECERS-R (Sylva et al., 2006; Soucacou & Sylva, 2010). It is generally accepted that when some new measure is developed, the measure should be tested for validity and reliability (Bryman & Cramer, 1996). Validity refers to the capacity of the new instrument to measure what it purports to measure—and not something else. In other words, a measure is valid if carrying out all its procedures leads to an accurate assessment of the idea or the concept it is trying to measure. Reliability refers to the consistency of a measure. There are two types of consistency: The first asks whether two or more observers would come up with the same score on the same day (consistency across observers) and the second concerns how the items relate to one another. The reliability and validity of the ECERS-E scale were established as follows:

Criterion Validity

A measure is said to have criterion validity if scores on it are very similar to scores on another, agreed instrument for measuring the same concept. Thus, criterion validity seeks agreement between a theoretical concept (what you are trying to measure) and a well-known measuring device or procedure that has been used successfully in the past (Bryman & Cramer, 1996). Criterion validity of the ECERS-E scale for the United Kingdom has been successfully demonstrated by a study of 141 preschool settings (Sylva et al., 1999; 2006). The correlation coefficient between total scores on the ECERS-R and the ECERS-E was 0.78, indicating a strong positive relationship between the two measures. Even though the two instruments focus on somewhat different dimensions of the preschool settings, they both measure a general construct of "quality." Therefore, it is expected that centers obtaining a high score on the ECERS-R will obtain a moderate-to-high score on the ECERS-E. However, there are still differences in what the two scales measure, and that is why the correlation is not 1.00, which would indicate that they measure exactly the same thing.

Apart from the high correlation between the ECERS-E and the ECERS-R, criterion validity of this new scale has also been established through the strong relationship with the Caregiver Interaction Scale (CIS), a scale for assessing the quality of relationships between setting staff and children. Sammons and colleagues (2002) report significant moderate correlations between the ECERS-E total and two CIS subscales: "positive relationship" (r = .59) and "detachment" (r = -.45). The correlation coefficients between all the ECERS-E subscales and the CIS subscales ranged from low to moderate, with the positive relationship subscale being moderately associated with all ECERS-E subscales (from .45 to .58).

Predictive Validity of the Construct (Children's Outcomes)

Predictive construct validity refers to the extent to which the scale predicts scores on some measure that can be theoretically deduced to relate to the new measure. For example, higher-quality centers should have children in them who make more developmental progress over time than centers with lower scores. In the case of the ECERS-E, quality scores of the centers correlated to greater developmental progress (gains between pre-test at age 3 and post-test at age 5) of children in the EPPE sample. The predictive power of the ECERS-E in relation to cognitive progress was found to be better than the ECERS-R in predicting progress of 3,000 children. Controlling for a large number of child, parent, family, home, and preschool characteristics, the ECERS-E total was significantly associated in a positive direction with pre-reading scores, early number concepts, and non-verbal reasoning. The literacy subscale had a significant positive correlation with both pre-reading and early number concepts. In addition, non-verbal reasoning was predicted by the math subscale of the ECERS-E and by the diversity subscale. The diversity subscale also had a significant positive correlation with early number concepts. As for behavioral outcomes, there was a trend (just missing significance at .05) for the ECERS-E to predict independence/concentration and co-operation/conformity (Sammons et al., 2003).

In an attempt to compare the size of the contribution of the ECERS-E and ECERS-R scores in predicting children's cognitive and social/behavioral outcomes, effect sizes were calculated following the method developed by Tymms, Merrell, & Henderson (1997). Effect sizes are important as they enable comparison of different predictors. These are presented in Table 1.

Table 1: Effect sizes of ECERS-R and ECERS-E total and subscale scores on cognitive and social/behavioral outcomes (after controlling for child, family, and home environment characteristics) (Sylva et al., 2006).

	COGNITIVE OUTCOMES					SOCIO-BEHAVIORAL OUTCOMES			
	Pre-reading	General Mathematical Concepts	Language	Non-verbal Reasoning	Spatial Awareness	Independence & Concentration	Cooperation & Conformity	Peer Sociability	Anti-social/ Worried
ECERS-E									
Total	0.166[a],*	0.163*	0.076	0.108*	0.023	0.120#	0.124#	0.073	-0.038
Literacy	0.174*	0.142*	0.059	0.105	-0.028	0.097	0.124#	0.077	-0.040
Math	0.127	0.102	0.042	0.142*	-0.041	0.054	0.077	0.090	0.028
Science/environment	0.012	0.105	0.091	0.109#	-0.056	0.111#	0.079	0.034	-0.059
Diversity	0.138#	0.165*	0.033	0.191*	-0.018	0.113#	0.117#	0.021	-0.046
ECERS-R									
Total	0.085	0.087	0.083	0.042	-0.044	0.089	0.131*	0.009	-0.094
Space and furnishings	0.068	0.008	0.065	0.022	-0.019	0.009	0.103	-0.033	-0.108
Personal care	-0.024	0.028	0.083	-0.057	0.042	0.055	0.128	0.026	-0.086
Language and reasoning	0.104	0.090	0.067	0.053	-0.108#	0.096	0.148*	0.030	-0.065
Activities	0.015	0.062	0.074	0.062	-0.065	0.046	0.067	-0.029	-0.028
Interaction	0.080	0.199*	0.053	0.073	-0.037	0.134*	0.180*	0.116#	-0.059
Program structure	0.063	0.035	0.041	0.037	-0.064	0.033	0.064	-0.018	-0.049
Parents and staff	0.144#	0.014	0.045	0.045	0.008	0.054	0.087	-0.012	-0.071

[a] When change of center is not included in the model; * $p<.05$; # $p<.08$

The significant and moderately strong relationship between the ECERS-E and children's cognitive development suggests that important elements of the educational/curricular environment measured in the ECERS-E scale are related to children's development. This, in turn, validates this instrument as a measure of quality related to "emerging" academic skills as well as social/behavioral development (Sylva et al., 2006).

The ECERS-R appears to be a more sensitive measure of quality related to children's social/behavioral development, while the ECERS-E better assesses quality relating to children's cognition and their "academic" skills. The fact that the two scales predict cognitive and social progress over the preschool period in different ways suggests that different aspects of children's development are being measured. Consequently, if academic achievement is valued at the start of school, then the ECERS-E is a good predictor of children's readiness for school (with regard to language, numeracy, and literacy skills). In a cultural context where the development of social skills is considered most important, then the ECERS-R is a better measure of a good start at school.

Concurrent Validity of the Construct (Qualifications of Staff)

Further criterion validity of the scale was established by examining the association between observed quality and the qualifications of staff. Theoretical considerations would predict that staff with higher qualifications would be found in centers with higher quality. Concurrent validity of the ECERS-E scale was established in the Millennium Cohort Study [MCS] (Mathers, Sylva, & Joshi, 2007). A random sample of 3-year-old children in the MCS who attended group care was selected, and the ECERS-R, ECERS-E, and CIS observations were carried out at those centers. Information on a number of center characteristics was collected, with the aim of establishing which center characteristics were related to, and thus predicted, high quality. The ECERS-E was used to measure the quality of provisions for literacy, math, science, diversity, and the overall quality of the environment. The childcare qualifications of center staff were an important predictor of ECERS-E scores in 301 centers in the MCS (Mathers & Sylva, 2007). Analyses revealed that, after controlling for a variety of center characteristics (including size, the ratio of children to staff, and type of center), the mean qualification level of all staff had a significant correlation to quality scores; it was significantly related to the total and to all subscales of the ECERS-E. The beta weights shown in Table 2 represent the degree to which staff qualifications in each of the 300+ centers predicted the ECERS-E scores.

Table 2: Relationship between mean staff qualifications and ECERS-E scores

ECERS-E subscale	Standardized ß	p value
Total ECERS-E score	0.21	< .001
Literacy	0.25	< .001
Math	0.15	< .05
Science	0.18	< .01
Diversity	0.13	< .05

The findings from the MCS suggest that the ECERS-E has concurrent validity. Qualifications were most strongly related to the literacy subscale of the ECERS-E, suggesting that higher qualifications are related more to literacy than to other aspects of the curriculum (Mathers & Sylva, 2007).

Inter-Rater Reliability

In the EPPE study (Sylva et al., 1999), inter-rater reliability on the ECERS-E was calculated from data obtained from the 25 randomly chosen centers that were also used in the factor analysis of the ECERS-R. The reliability coefficients were calculated separately for different regions of the country, both percentages of exact agreement between the raters and as a weighted kappa coefficient. The percentages of inter-rater agreement range from 88.4 to 97.6, and the kappas range from 0.83 to 0.97, indicating very high levels of agreement between raters. Similar high levels of agreement were found in the study conducted by Mathers and Sylva (2007).

Factor Analysis and Internal Consistency

Factor analysis conducted on the ECERS-E in 141 centers (Sylva et al., 2006) indicated the presence of two factors that together account for about 50% of the total variance in the scores. The first factor has been named Curriculum and the second Diversity. Table 3 presents the items that load (higher than .6) on these two factors.

Table 3: Two factors in the ECERS-E (N = 141 centers)

Factor 1: Curriculum	Loading	Factor 2: Diversity	Loading
Environmental Print: letters and words	0.684	Gender equality	0.763
Natural materials	0.683	Race equality	0.702
Counting	0.678	Book and literacy areas	0.643
Science resourcing	0.656		
Talking and listening	0.649		
Sounds in words	0.634		

A Cronbach's alpha was calculated for each factor: This was high (0.84) for factor 1 and moderate (0.64) for factor 2. The alpha values show that the two factors have moderate to good internal consistency.

Scores on the Validating Sample on ECERS-R and ECERS-E

The mean total score from the 141 centers on the ECERS-R was 4.34 (SD = 1.00) and 3.07 (SD = 1.00) on the ECERS-E. The former score is in the "adequate to good" range while the latter indicates "adequate" quality. Table 4 shows the total and subscale score on both scales.

Table 4: Total and subscale scores on ECERS-R and ECERS-E from the validation sample (n = 141 preschool centers; Sylva et al., 2006)

	Mean	SD
ECERS-R		
1. Space and furnishings	4.85	1.04
2. Personal care routines	3.81	1.36
3. Language and reasoning	4.32	1.33
4. Activities	3.83	1.16
5. Interaction	4.82	1.31
6. Program structure	4.70	1.47
7. Parents and Staff	4.07	1.28
Total ECERS-R	4.34	1.00
ECERS-E		
1. Literacy	3.96	1.06
2. Mathematics	2.95	1.19
3. Science and environment	2.98	1.52
4. Diversity	2.38	1.11
Total ECERS-E	3.07	1.01

Quality Across Nations and Cultures

The concept of "quality" is not universal; it is influenced by national curricula and cultural priorities. The outcomes thought to be important in children's development will relate in different ways to different measures of quality. If academic achievement is valued at the start of school, then the ECERS-E is a good predictor of children's readiness for school. This readiness includes language, numeracy skills, the component skills of early literacy, and scientific understanding. However, if social outcomes are valued, then the social interaction scale on the ECERS-R may be a better predictor of a child's strong start at school. The social outcomes related most to the ECERS-R were children's independence and cooperation/conformity.

The ECERS-E was developed in England, although its structure was influenced greatly by the ECERS-R, developed in the United States. It has proved valid in other European countries (e.g., Rossbach, in preparation), and we welcome discussion with those who use it for research or professional development around the world.

References

Audit Commission. (1996). *Counting to five*. London: Author.

Ball, C. (1994) *Start right: the importance of early learning*. London: Royal Society of Arts, Manufacturing and Commerce.

Bredekamp, S., & Copple, C. (Eds.). (1997). *Developmentally Appropriate Practice in early childhood programs*. Washington, DC: National Association for the Education of Young Children.

Bryman, A., & Cramer, D. (1996). *Quantitative data analysis with minitab: A guide for social scientists*. London: Routledge.

Cryer, D., Harms, T., & Riley, C. (2003). *All about the ECERS-R*. Lewisville, NC: Pact House Publishing.

Department of Education and Skills. (1990). *Starting with quality: Report of the committee of inquiry into the quality of educational experiences offered to 3 and 4-year-olds* [Rumbold Report]. London: Her Majesty's Stationery Office.

Department for Education and Skills. (2007a). *The early years foundation stage: Setting the standards for learning, development and care for children from birth to five*. Nottingham, U.K.: Author.

Department for Education and Skills. (2007b). *Statutory framework for the early years foundation stage*. Nottingham, U.K.: Author.

Evangelou, M., Sylva, K., Kyriacou, M., Wild, M., & Glenny, G. (2009). *Early years learning and development: literature review*. London: Department for Children, Schools and Families.

Harms, T., Clifford, R. M., & Cryer, D. (2003). *Infant/toddler environment rating scale–Revised (ITERS-R)*. New York: Teachers College Press.

Harms, T., Clifford, R. M., & Cryer, D. (2005). *Early childhood environment rating scale–Revised (ECERS-R)* New York: Teachers College Press.

Harms, T., & Cryer, D. (2006). *Video Observations for the ECERS-R*. New York: Teachers College Press.

Harms, T., Cryer, D., & Clifford, R. M. (2007). *Family child care environment rating scale–Revised (FCCERS-R)*. New York: Teachers College Press.

Harms, T., Jacobs., E. V., & White. D. R. (1996). *School-age care environment rating scale (SACERS)*. New York: Teachers College Press.

Ilsley, B. J. (2000) *The Tamil Nadu early childhood environmental rating scale (TECERS)*. Chennai, India: M.S. Swaminathan Research Foundation.

Mason, J. M., & Stewart, J. P. (1990). Emergent literacy assessment for instructional use in kindergarten. In L. M. Morrow & J. K. Smith (Eds.), *Assessment for instruction in early literacy* (pp. 155–175). Englewood Cliffs, NJ: Prentice-Hall.

Mathers, S., & Linskey, F. (Forthcoming). *All about the ECERS-E*.

Mathers, S., Linskey, F., Seddon, J., & Sylva, K. (2007). Using quality rating scales for professional development: experiences from the U.K. *International Journal of Early Years Education, 15*(3), 261–274. Available at http://dx.doi.org/10.1080/09669760701516959

Mathers, S., & Sylva, K. (2007). *National Evaluation of the Neighbourhood Nurseries Initiative: The Relationship between Quality and Children's Behavioural Development* [Sure Start Research Report SSU/2007/FR/022]. London: DfES/Department of Educational Studies, University of Oxford.

Mathers, S., Sylva, K., & Joshi, H. (2007). *Quality of childcare settings in the Millennium Cohort Study* [DSCF Research report SSU/2008/FR-025]. London: DCSF.

Office for Standards in Education (Ofsted). (2008). *Early years self-evaluation form guidance: Guidance to support using the self-evaluation form to evaluate the quality of registered early years provision and ensure continuous improvement* [Reference No 080103]. London: Author. Available at www.ofsted.gov.uk.

Qualification and Curriculum Authority. (2000). *Curriculum guidance for the foundation stage*. London: Qualifications and Curriculum Authority.

Qualification and Curriculum Authority & Department for Education and Skills. (2003). *The foundation stage profile*. London: Qualifications and Curriculum Authority Publications.

Rogoff, B., & Lave, J. (Eds.). (1999). *Everyday cognition: Its development in social context*. Cambridge, MA: Harvard University Press.

Rossbach, H. G. (in preparation). *Using the ECERS-R in German pre-school centers*.

Sammons, P., Sylva, K., Melhuish, E., Siraj-Blatchford, I., Taggart, B., & Elliot, K. (2002). *Measuring the impact of pre-school on children's cognitive progress over the pre-school period* [Technical Paper 8a]. London: Institute of Education.

Sammons, P., Sylva, K., Melhuish, E., Siraj-Blatchford, I., Taggart, B., & Elliot, K. (2003). *Measuring the impact of pre-school on children's social behavioural development over the pre-school period* [Technical Paper 8b]. London: Institute of Education.

Senechal, M., Lefevre, J.-A., Smith-Chant, B. L., & Colton, K. V. (2001). On refining theoretical models of emergent literacy: The role of empirical evidence. *Journal of School Psychology, 39*(5), 439–460.

Siraj-Blatchford, I. (2002a). *Final annual evaluation report of the Gamesley Early Excellence Center*. Unpublished report, University of London, Institute of Education.

Siraj-Blatchford, I. (2002b). *Final annual evaluation report of the Thomas Coram Early Excellence Center*. Unpublished report, University of London, Institute of Education.

Siraj-Blatchford, I., Sylva, K., Muttock, S., Gilden, R. & Bell, D. (2002). *Researching Effective Pedagogy in the Early Years (REPEY) study*. London: DfES Publications.

Siraj-Blatchford, I., Sylva, K., Taggart, B., Sammons, P., Melhuish, E. C., & Elliot, K. (2003). *The Effective Provision of Pre-School Education (EPPE) Project: Technical Paper 10—Intensive case studies of practice across the foundation stage* [DfES Research Brief No. RBX 16-03, October 2003]. Nottingham: DfES Publications.

Snow, C. E. (2006). What counts as literacy in early childhood? In K. McCartney & D. Phillips (Eds.), *Blackwell handbook of early childhood development* (pp. 274–294). Malden, MA: Blackwell.

Soucacou, E., & Sylva, K. (2010). Developing observation instruments and arriving at inter-rater reliability for a range of contexts and raters: The early childhood environment rating scales. In G. Walford, E. Tucker. & M. Viswanathan (Eds.), *The Sage handbook of measurement* (pp. 61–85). London: Sage Publications.

Storch, S. A., & Whitehurst, G. J. (2001). The role of family and home in the literacy development of children from low-income backgrounds. *New Directions For Child and Adolescent Development, 92*, 53–71.

Sulzby, E., & Teale, W. (1991). Emergent literacy. In R. Barr, M. Kamil, P. Mosenthal, & P. D. Pearson (Eds.), *Handbook of reading research* (Vol. 2, pp. 727–758). New York: Longman.

Sylva, K., Melhuish, E., Sammons, P., Siraj-Blatchford, I., & Taggart, B. (2004). *The Effective Provision of Pre-school Education (EPPE) project: Final report* [A longitudinal study funded by the DfES 1997–2003]. Nottingham: Department for Children, Schools and Families.

Sylva, K., Melhuish, E., Sammons, P., Siraj-Blatchford, I., & Taggart, B. (2008). *Final report from the primary phase: Pre-school, school and family influences on children's development during Key Stage 2 (age 7–11)* [DCSF RR 061]. Nottingham: Department for Children, Schools and Families.

Sylva, K., Melhuish, E., Sammons, P., Siraj-Blatchford, I., & Taggart, B. (2010). *Early childhood matters.* New York and London: Routledge Taylor Francis Group.

Sylva, K., Siraj-Blatchford, I., Melhuish, E., Sammons, P., Taggart, B., Evans, E., Dobson, A., Jeavons, M., Lewis, K., Morahan, M., & Sadler, S. (1999). *Characteristics of the centers in the EPPE sample: Observational profiles* (Technical Paper 6). London: Institute of Education.

Sylva, K., Siraj-Blatchford, I, Taggart, B., Sammons, P., Melhuish, E., Elliot, K, & Totsika V. (2006). Capturing quality in early childhood through environmental rating scales. *Early Childhood Research Quarterly, 21*, 76–92.

Tietze, W., Cryer, D., Bairrao, J., Palacios, J., & Wetzel, G. (1996). Comparisons of observed process quality of early child care and education in five countries. *Early Childhood Research Quarterly, 11*(4), 447–475.

Tymms, P., Merrell, C., & Henderson, B. (1997). The first year at school: A quantitative investigation of the attainment and progress of pupils. *Educational Research and Evaluation, 3*(2), 101–118.

Whitehurst, G. J., & Lonigan, C. J. (1998). Child development and emergent literacy. *Child Development, 69*(3), 848–872.

Wood, D., Bruner, J. S., & Ross, G. (1976). The role of tutoring in problem solving. *Journal of Child Psychology and Psychiatry, 17*(2), 89–100.

Yan Yan, L., & Yuejuan, P. (2008). Development and validation of kindergarten environment rating scale. *International Journal of Early Years Education, 16*(2), 101–114.

NOTES

NOTES